YOU CAN DO IT YOURSELF
INVESTORS GUIDE

How to Invest In Your 401K and IRA

CHARLIE EMERY

iUniverse, Inc.
Bloomington

YOU CAN DO IT YOURSELF INVESTORS GUIDE
HOW TO INVEST IN YOUR 401K AND IRA

Copyright © 2013 Charlie Emery.

All rights reserved. No part of this book may be used or reproduced by any means, graphic, electronic, or mechanical, including photocopying, recording, taping or by any information storage retrieval system without the written permission of the publisher except in the case of brief quotations embodied in critical articles and reviews.

The information, ideas, and suggestions in this book are not intended to render professional advice. Before following any suggestions contained in this book, you should consult your personal accountant or other financial advisor. Neither the author nor the publisher shall be liable or responsible for any loss or damage allegedly arising as a consequence of your use or application of any information or suggestions in this book.

iUniverse books may be ordered through booksellers or by contacting:

iUniverse
1663 Liberty Drive
Bloomington, IN 47403
www.iuniverse.com
1-800-Authors (1-800-288-4677)

Because of the dynamic nature of the Internet, any web addresses or links contained in this book may have changed since publication and may no longer be valid. The views expressed in this work are solely those of the author and do not necessarily reflect the views of the publisher, and the publisher hereby disclaims any responsibility for them.

Any people depicted in stock imagery provided by Thinkstock are models, and such images are being used for illustrative purposes only.

Certain stock imagery © Thinkstock.

ISBN: 978-1-4759-7743-1 (sc)
ISBN: 978-1-4759-7742-4 (hc)
ISBN: 978-1-4759-7741-7 (e)

Library of Congress Control Number: 2013903335

Printed in the United States of America

iUniverse rev. date: 4/4/2013

To My Wonderful Wife Betty:

Thank you for helping me get through the trial and error of writing my first book. I'm truly blessed for having had you by my side for the last forty-eight years. I love you.

TABLE OF CONTENTS

Introduction ix
CHAPTER 1 Why You Should Just Do It Yourself. 1
CHAPTER 2 Investing in Your Employer's Plan 11
CHAPTER 3 Mutual Funds 19
CHAPTER 4 The Business Cycle 25
CHAPTER 5 Beat The Market With Exchange Traded Funds 37
CHAPTER 6 Beat the Market With Dividend Paying Common Stocks...49
CHAPTER 7 Master Limited Partnerships (MLPs) 81
CHAPTER 8 Fixed Income 91
CHAPTER 9 A Little Speculation 97
CHAPTER 10 Alternative Investments 107
Afterword 111
Index..113

INTRODUCTION

I've always been a 'do it yourself' type of person. You have probably heard about that old adage: "A jack of all trades is the master of none". That being said, most people are capabable of being very good at more than one thing. So, I'll let you know right now that I have never worked in the financial services industry, and I don't have any recognized professional credentials or letters after my name. I'm an accountant who recently retired (in 2009).

There are some advantages to not having worked in the financial services industry, and being a sixty-seven year old retiree who wants to share the investing knowledge he has gained through many years of trial and error. There isn't the worry about a boss looking at my book and asking: "**Why *did you write that?*"** Nothing is being held back that might benefit you. I'm free to speak from the heart. In writing this book there isn't any hidden agenda. The main goal is that you will benefit from what you read and recommend this book to your friends and colleagues. Hopefully, you will believe this book is worth at least as much as a one year subscription to a financially oriented magazine. This book is written from the individual investor's perspective because, to be honest, it's the only perspective I've ever experienced.

If you bought this book looking for a guru that promises to make you a millionaire overnight, you bought the wrong book. If you bought this book because you are tired of hearing financial planners and investment advisors promise you big returns, but still want their high fees even when they don't deliver on their promises, you have taken at least one step towards that goal.

Another main goal is that you, after reading this book, will want to fire your financial advisor if you still have one. Are you familiar with (or willing to learn) a spreadsheet software program like Excel? Are you willing to spend a few hours each week managing your own investments? In addition, are you willing to follow a disciplined plan of action? It's assumed that you are, and this book will help you plan your financial future and manage those investments yourself. Don't let this task scare you.

Henry Ford was once quoted as saying:

'If you think you can or — *can't*—you are right'.

It mostly comes down to your desire to succeed, and no one cares more about your financial future than *you* do.

Back in the early 1990's I started saving in my 401k plan at work. I also had a regular IRA account (Roth IRAs were not available then) with a major full service brokerage. After I noticed that this company's mutual funds were not keeping pace with market returns, my broker told me I shouldn't expect to match the market returns with his company's mutual funds. Instead I should let him pick good stocks for me. So I followed his advice on a couple of stocks and did not get good results. Against that brokers advice, I went with my own knowledge of Ford Motor Company (F) stock and Chrysler Bonds (I worked for Chrysler for over forty-four years). We were coming out of the recession in the early 1990's. I got much better results than this so called financial professional by going against his advice. He did not have a good enough explanation for me so I moved on to a discount broker and I have never looked back.

I'm an amateur investor who has tried to work hard and learn from my mistakes, and I've achieved much better than average results. I have been actively managing my own portfolios since the early 1990s and I've found that just as in anything else we do in life, there is a learning curve involved in investing. It's not that difficult if you a willing to follow a few simple rules and learn from your mistakes or, better yet, the mistakes of others, and most of all, if you don't let the naysayers scare you. I am especially proud of the results I have achieved since January 1, 1999. That's fourteen calendar years and counting. I've made all of my buy and sell decisions since the early 1990s including investing in:

Mutual Funds
Exchange Traded Funds (ETF's)
Common Stocks
Master Limited Partnerships (MLPs)
Corporate Bonds
Preferred Stocks

Now, if after reading this book and learning whatever you can from other sources (which is highly recommend) you decide that managing your own investments is not for you for whatever reason, I would strongly suggest you find a *fee only* financial planner. This would be someone who should be working for you only and not receiving commissions from other sources.

When you have a stock broker, especially from a major brokerage firm, his or her only obligation to you is to recommend a *suitable* investment. For example, there could be a situation where there are ten mutual funds to choose from, and the advisor recommends the worst performing fund which just happens to pay him the biggest commission. The broker is untroubled since the fund can still be considered *suitable* but purchasing it is not necessarily in your best interest. A financial advisor is held to a higher standard, he or she is obligated to *act in your best interest and pick the best available fund for you.*

Now in the decade to come, if we were to invest the way we should be investing in the current decade it's very unlikely that we would get the same results. One of the main goals of this book is to help you understand the trend we are in, and learn to spot different trends as they present themselves in the future. Keep in mind that we are focusing on long term investing.

INVEST
IN YOURSELF

CHAPTER ONE
WHY YOU SHOULD JUST DO IT YOURSELF.

There are a lot of reasons for managing your own investments and they can't all be listed. There are literally enough examples to fill a book on just that subject. But here are few so that you get the idea:

Defined benefit pensions—that is pensions that pay you a monthly benefit starting when you retire and pay you for the rest of your life are fast becoming obsolete. Since 1979 the percentage of workers enrolled in defined benefit pension have gone steadily down, while those in '*defined contribution*' plans has gone steadily up. With the defined contribution plans (i.e. 401k/403b) you have to either make the investment decisions yourself, or hire someone to do it for you.

For example, a friend I'll call Tom went to work for a major pharmaceutical company in the 1960s. He retired in the early 1990s with a nice pension and health care. He passed away a few years ago, but his wife Mary still enjoys a portion of his pension as well as health care from his company. A somewhat younger friend, John, went to work for the same company in the early 2000s. All he was offered was a 401k plan with a 3% match of the first 6% that he contributed.

Whenever there is a change like this, most employees will not benefit as much because of it. However, those who learn how to invest intelligently can do very well. The future is always uncertain, and for the people who want to take total control of their financial future this can be a time of great opportunity.

Investing has been made easier for the individual investor over the years if you look past all the fluff. Over the last twenty years we have been given the Roth IRA, lower brokerage fees if you use a discount broker,

Exchange Traded Funds (ETFs) that track major indexes, and lower fees on some traditional (mostly index) mutual funds.

ETFs resemble mutual funds in many ways. One, they are a pool of assets such as stocks and/or bonds that can change from day to day as the manager sees fit. They can also use futures in some cases. In most cases they track an index. Unlike mutual funds, ETFs can be bought and sold throughout the trading day. ETFs will be discussed much more in the following chapters.

The Internet is your friend. You can use Yahoo Finance (yahoo.com) to keep track of all the exchange traded funds (ETFs), common stocks, preferred stocks, and the indexes that you want to follow. Using Yahoo without paying them a fee, I track eight different portfolios with at least one-hundred issues. MSN Money is also a valuable source of information. You can find a lot of good commentary on MSN Money, as well as ten years worth of financial information on most major publicly traded companies. Both Yahoo and MSN Money also have charts that you can use to compare stocks, ETFs etc.

The 'Bonds Screener' on Yahoo Finance is a very good website to look for corporate bonds that you might want to invest in. I find it very easy to use, and from it you can get all the preliminary information you need to start your bond research.

You should have at least two brokerage accounts, with different discount brokers, and most all brokerages have a lot of useful information on their websites. There are a lot of great websites that you can find on Google. Your stock trading should be done on line, because it is very easy and the least expensive way to trade. You should have one account for your 401k/403b and a different one for your Roth IRA. You would need a third one, if you are able to move money from a previous employer to a regular IRA. It's better to have a regular IRA at one discount broker, and a Roth IRA at another discount broker. This will keep you from mixing your apples and oranges, because you will have to treat each account differently for tax purposes. In these trying economic times there could be another meltdown at one of your financial institutions, and as a result you would still have access to your money at the other.

You can withdraw funds from your Roth IRA before age 59 ½, up to $10,000 to purchase a first home or pay college tuition costs. For the 2013 tax year you are eligible to contribute to a Roth IRA, as long as your adjusted gross income (AGI) is not over $112,000 if you are single or

$178,000 for a married couple filing a joint return. If your income exceeds these amounts, your contribution is phased out completely at $127,000 and $188,000 respectively. Please check with your tax advisor, or go to the IRS website (irs.gov) and see Publication 590 for the latest information. As always, these rules are subject to change. These amounts are adjusted for inflation each year, and the new limits are usually announced in October prior to the New Year beginning. This way you have a tax deferred as well a tax free account, which will give you maximum tax flexibility after you retire. Currently, for 2013 you can contribute $5,500 per year to your Roth IRA and an additional $1,000 if you are over fifty years of age for a total of $6,500 per year. You also will have until April 15, 2014 to make IRA contributions for the 2013 tax year. These amounts will also be adjusted for inflation in future years under current law. With your discount brokerage account you will have **more choice, more control, and lower fees** than with your 401k/403b.

According to the non-profit 'Center for Responsive Politics', a group that tracks influence peddling, there are twenty-eight officially registered lobbyists for each member of Congress working in Washington, DC today. They are spending at least $3.5 billion annually on lobbying. A good percentage are working on financial industry regulation, or should I say **de-regulation**. Does anyone believe that any more than a very few of them are working in the individual investor's best interest? It's not likely.

One would think that the major Wall Street brokerages would always have been a big promoter of the free enterprise system, especially in their own industry. Not true, broker commissions were fixed until the 1970s and the major brokerages were dragged kicking and screaming to the more competitive system we have today. As a result in the 1950s the average share of stock on the New York Stock Exchange (NYSE) only changed hands once every six years. Now, in the second decade of the twenty-first century the average holding period is about nine months. Now with commissions much lower, many in the brokerage industry are trying to make day traders out of us so they can make up for those lost commissions.

Day trading is the practice of speculation in all types of financial securities by buying and selling within the same trading day. Many brokerage firms encourage the practice by offering sophisticated technical analysis software. Most day traders close their positions by the end of the trading day. This practice has become more and more popular with individual investors trading from their home. (More about this practice in Chapter Ten)

A recent United States Supreme Court decision handed down said that mutual fund investment advisors can't be held liable under federal securities laws, for false statements made by the funds they advise, because they are "separate legal entities".

As for the Securities and Exchange Commission (SEC), are they going to protect us? Remember the financial meltdown of 2008? What about the Bernie Madoff fiasco and Enron? There is a whole TV series about financial rip-offs on CNBC called *'American Greed'*. You should watch a few episodes, if you haven't already, and you will get the idea.

Now let's dream a little. Let's say you just hit the lottery or received a big inheritance, or sold your business and are ready to enjoy the fruits of your labor and you net $5,000,000 and found a good honest financial advisor. Now with your good fortune, let's say you decide you are never going to work another day as long as you live. Conventional wisdom, regardless of your age, would say you should start by withdrawing 4% or $200,000 the first year, and adjust your withdrawal each year by the inflation rate the previous year. A 3% inflation rate would dictate $206,000 in year two, and $212,180 in year three, etc.

Now let me introduce you to *"Financial Advisor Math"*. A typical advisor will want to charge you at least "1% of assets under their management", or $50,000 per year. By my math that looks like at least 25% of your yearly withdrawal before you pay any taxes, or 30-35% of you're after tax withdrawal from your account. Your advisor would only have to find three or four more clients like yourself, and he or she would have hit the lottery without even buying a lottery ticket.

Here is a more likely example of *"Financial Advisor Math"*. On smaller amounts of money like your 401k/403b, or IRA the typical advisor will want to charge you "only" 1.25% per year of assets under their management, automatically deducted from your account quarterly. Here is the bad part. That fee is coming out of your account even if they mismanage your money, and your account goes down while the market is going up. Even if you are getting the typical 10.00% per year return, the advisor is taking 12.5% of your earnings on your account each and every year. Look at Spreadsheets 1.1 and 1.2, and you will see how much this can add up to on a modest portfolio over a twenty year period. On just a

$5,000 per contribution per year and a 10.00% return per year, you could be paying your advisor over $24,000 but your nest egg would be more than $48,000 higher if you managed it yourself due to compounding.

There is one person (there are most likely many others) who has an account with a major brokerage firm that charges the typical 1% of assets under their management each year, and if he makes his own decision to buy an issue he is still charged an additional $200 for the transaction. Example: For a $10,000 issue this is a 3.00% commission verses 0.10% for a typical $10 commission at a discount broker. Add that up over time, and there is plenty of incentive to do the investing yourself, even when you make a few mistakes, you have a very good chance to come out ahead in the long run.

Are advisors from the major brokerages going to beat the market for you after they take out their commissions and fees? I have serious doubt that very many can. A commissioned planner or advisor is usually under pressure to make a sales quota, and to sell financial products that are being underwritten by their firm. As 2004 Democratic Vice Presidential candidate John Edwards recently said: *"I did a lot wrong but I didn't do anything illegal"*. In this instance one would have to believe his statement was the absolute truth. With all the lobbyists in Washington today, the people they are looking out for the most are Wall Street and the politicians themselves. Unfortunately that's the legal environment we live in today. We must look out for ourselves because our government isn't likely to.

Theoretically, we have the Financial Industry Regulatory Authority (FINRA) to protect us from Wall Street mischief. This is the brokerage industry's self regulator. If you were to be victimized by someone in the financial services industry, and you take them to arbitration and you are fortunate enough to win, the typical recovery rate is about 20% of the original claim. As with most any industry self regulation, it's very hard to tell the difference from *no* regulation at all. The fact of the matter is that Wall Street interests are going to be opposed to any and all regulatory improvements that benefits individual investors like us. We have to look out for ourselves and just not trust the greedy bastards.

In addition, you are bound to have heard of diploma mills before. If you send in a little (lot of) money to someone you can have a doctorate degree in whatever field you want to pass yourself off as an expert in. These same people (or their friends) are in the business of giving out awards for financial expertise. So buyers beware. Also, keep in mind that neither the SEC nor FINRA endorses any professional designation. Now, you shouldn't demean what are considered two of the more prestigious designations, which are "Chartered Financial Analyst" (CFA) and "Certified Public Accountant" (CPA). To obtain either of these certifications, one must go through a rigorous training program and pass a tough, multi-part exam.

Barron's is a weekly publication that is filled with a lot of valuable information that you should not want to miss out on each week. Every few weeks they put in a section on the one hundred top financial advisors. They tell us about the net worth of their clients, whether they are rich, very rich, or super rich. Then they rate them on some other criteria that's not the most relevant. Why don't they tell us what we really want to know about these advisors? How about what kind of returns they have been getting for the last one, three, five and ten year periods? And by the way, how do their returns compare to that of the market during that same period? Needless to say, you shouldn't pay too much attention to that section when it is published. It seems like they want to tell us everything **but** what we really want to know.

There is hope once you learn where to look for it. There is the semi-annual Barron's—Zack's ranking of brokers' stock pick lists. This is a rare opportunity to see money managers from the big money management firms ranked to each other by a third party. Their returns are measured on six months, one year, three years and five years every January 1, and July 1 and results are published about four weeks after the period ends in Barron's.

If you still need a little more convincing that many financial newsletters fudge their results on the high side, you should subscribe to Hulbert's Financial Digest for a year. This publication has been tracking most investment newsletters for the past thirty years. This publication gives the best unbiased measure of performance in the financial services industry.

Yr	Spreadsheet 1.1 Begin Total	Contri-bution	Grand Total	1.25% Fee	Amount Invested	10.00% Return Yr End
1	0	5,000	5,000	63	4,938	5,431
2	5,431	5,000	10,431	130	10,301	11,331
3	11,331	5,000	16,331	204	16,127	17,739
4	17,739	5,000	22,739	284	22,455	24,701
5	24,701	5,000	29,701	371	29,330	32,262
6	32,262	5,000	37,262	466	36,797	40,476
7	40,476	5,000	45,476	568	44,908	49,399
8	49,399	5,000	54,399	680	53,719	59,091
9	59,091	5,000	64,091	801	63,289	69,618
10	69,618	5,000	74,618	933	73,686	81,054
11	81,054	5,000	86,054	1,076	84,979	93,476
12	93,476	5,000	98,476	1,231	97,245	106,970
13	106,970	5,000	111,970	1,400	110,570	121,627
14	121,627	5,000	126,627	1,583	125,045	137,549
15	137,549	5,000	142,549	1,782	140,767	154,844
16	154,844	5,000	159,844	1,998	157,846	173,630
17	173,630	5,000	178,630	2,233	176,398	194,037
18	194,037	5,000	199,037	2,488	196,549	216,204
19	216,204	5,000	221,204	2,765	218,439	240,283
20	240,283	5,000	245,283	3,066	242,217	**266,439**
		100,000		24,122		

Yr	Spreadsheet 1.2 Begin Total	Contri-bution	Grand Total	1.25% Fee	Amount Invested	10.00% Return Yr End
1	0	5,000	5,000	0	5,000	5,500
2	5,500	5,000	10,500	0	10,500	11,550
3	11,550	5,000	16,550	0	16,550	18,205
4	18,205	5,000	23,205	0	23,205	25,526
5	25,526	5,000	30,526	0	30,526	33,578
6	33,578	5,000	38,578	0	38,578	42,436
7	42,436	5,000	47,436	0	47,436	52,179
8	52,179	5,000	57,179	0	57,179	62,897
9	62,897	5,000	67,897	0	67,897	74,687
10	74,687	5,000	79,687	0	79,687	87,656
11	87,656	5,000	92,656	0	92,656	101,921
12	101,921	5,000	106,921	0	106,921	117,614
13	117,614	5,000	122,614	0	122,614	134,875
14	134,875	5,000	139,875	0	139,875	153,862
15	153,862	5,000	158,862	0	158,862	174,749
16	174,749	5,000	179,749	0	179,749	197,724
17	197,724	5,000	202,724	0	202,724	222,996
18	222,996	5,000	227,996	0	227,996	250,795
19	250,795	5,000	255,795	0	255,795	281,375
20	281,375	5,000	286,375	0	286,375	315,012
		100,000		0	$ Gain	48,573
					% Gain	15.42%

CHAPTER TWO
INVESTING IN YOUR EMPLOYER'S PLAN

Let's get to the basics. Hopefully you have a 401k or 403b plan with your employer with a company match. As you probably already know, many employers sponsored 401k/403b plans are not noted for their array of investment choices. Unfortunately, many of the smaller plans have just mutual funds. They also tend to have higher fees, but with the tax deferred benefits of these plans about all you can do is grin and bear it. Unfortunately for us, the traditional mutual fund industry has a lot of very good sales people that sold these plans to your employer and stuck you with the high fees and limited choices.

Keep in mind, as a general rule the smaller the employer plan you are in the higher the fees and fewer the choices tend to be. According to Smart Money magazine's August 2012 issue: A recent study found that workers in plans with less than $1 million in plan assets paid an average of $141 in fees per $10,000 invested. This is more than triple the fees that the larger plans charge. This is due in a large part to economies of scale.

There is good news for some of the larger plans. As reported in Smart Money magazine in June 2012: According to the Plan Sponsor Council of America (PSCA) about one in five employers offers a self-directed option in which workers can invest in stocks and bonds.

For most plans in 2013 you can contribute up to $17,500 per year in most 401k / 403b plans and an additional $5,500 per year if you are over fifty years old for a total of $23,000 per year. The total employer and employee match can't exceed $51,000 for 2013. These amounts will be adjusted for inflation in future years under current law. These inflation adjustments are usually published in October prior to the New Year. This will help you to plan ahead. You should put these estimates on your spreadsheet and adjust your percentage contribution as necessary throughout the year.

Whatever amount you can afford to save, let's hope it's enough to get *the entire* employer match. A typical plan might be if you contribute 8% you will get the full company match of 3%. This typical example is like getting a 37.5% return the first year. This should be your first priority, to contribute *just enough* to get the full company match and not any more just yet. If you're a higher salaried employee you don't want to max out your contribution before your last paycheck at the end of the year because, typically, your employer match will also stop. This could easily cost you over $1,200 per year in employer matching funds in a typical plan. You want to get the maximum benefit out of your employer's match. Look at Spreadsheets 2.1 and 2.2 for a typical example.

Now that we have your 401k/403b contributions figured out, what should we do with the *next funds* you are saving for retirement? Next, you should open up a Roth IRA account, if you are eligible, with a discount broker. Why a Roth? Because we don't know for sure what the future of tax rates are going to be, but they will in all probability go up. Roth IRAs are funded with after tax funds and the earnings won't be taxed in the future under current law.

Now, after you have planned your funding for your (and your spouse's) Roth IRA, and if you are fortunate enough to be able to save even more you can go back and finish funding your 401k/403b, but remember to take the whole calendar year to do so. You don't want to lose any of your employer's matching funds. Remember this funding, as much as possible, should be planned and laid out on your spreadsheets in December *before* the New Year starts. You can make adjustments to your percent saved if your income changes during the year from what you forecasted.

If you have changed jobs recently, most employer plans will allow you to roll over the money from your old 401k/403b plan to the new employer's plan. But that does *not* mean you should do so. In fact I strongly advise *against* doing so. If your goal is *more choice, more control* **and lower fees**, then this is your golden opportunity to achieve this goal of getting as much control of your assets as possible. You should roll over your old plan into a *Regular IRA,* with a discount broker, which will be tax deferred just like the employer plans, but will leave you with much more control.

If your employer plan allows you to purchase common stocks, that is a very good tool if used properly. Are you having $100 to $200 or so withheld each pay period, and are using these funds to purchase one to five shares of a stock each pay period? If so, this method (dollar cost averaging) is *not* likely going to work well for you. If you are buying stock this way, check to see how much commission you are paying. Add this up for about ten pay periods including the **commissions.** Chances are unless the stock is in the middle of a huge run up; you would be better off putting your contribution in cash temporarily, and purchasing the stock at most once or twice per year. Your Human Resources person or plan administrator might have made dollar cost averaging sound good. Buying stock like this in the employer plans is usually only best for the ones that are collecting the commissions. There will be more on this in Chapter Six on stock investing.

Good news, (maybe): If you are age 59 ½ or older and still working, you may be able to roll over all or part of your employer plan (401k/403b) into a Regular IRA, and still continue make current year contributions as long as you are still working. This is also known as an 'In Service Withdrawal'. According to Smart Money magazine's June 2012 issue, 86% of employer plans with more than 5,000 participants permit this. I was able to do this myself back in 2005. Check with your plan administrator. If by chance your plan permits this they are not likely to go out of their way to make this known to you. It's highly recommend that this be done if your plan allows this. You could quite possibly be required to sell part or even all of your investments in your employer plan in order to do the transfer. I had to sell everything which at that time included ETFs and stocks. If you are in one of those plans that only have mutual funds in them, this is a golden opportunity to get a head start on how you will be investing in your retirement years. If and when you do decide to do this, try to pick a time of market stability.

Now, on to those dreaded mutual funds that we must deal with. The best mutual fund that I'm aware of that is available in some employer plans is the Vanguard S&P 500 Index Fund (VFINX). It was one of the first S&P 500 Index mutual funds to come out in 1976. It has a very good track record of mirroring the S&P 500 Index. It has outperformed most all mutual funds that have been in existence since then. It is available in many plans and it has a very low (0.17%) expense ratio. First, take a good look and see what is available in your plan. Hopefully, your plan offers an S&P 500 Index fund with a very low expense rate. Next, there probably is a mid cap or small cap index fund. Index funds tend to offer lower expense ratios than those (and I use the term loosely) professionally managed funds. It's been proven that in most cases index funds outperform the professionally managed funds. Whenever possible, stick with the lower expense index funds. If your plan offers an index 'Exchange Traded Fund' (ETF) option, it is in all probability the best way to invest.

Mid cap and small cap stocks tend to perform very closely the same as a group. I prefer the small cap funds because there are usually more to choose from. If you decide to invest in a small cap fund for the long term, choose one that mirrors the 'S&P 600 Small Cap Index' rather than the 'Russell 2000 Small Cap Index', if you have a choice. Even though they are both small cap indexes they have different criteria and the S&P 600 has historically been by far the better performer over the long term.

According to my personal records from January 1, 2001 through December 31, 2012 the S&P 600 Small Cap Index exchange traded fund (IJR) has outperformed the Russell 2000 Small Cap Index exchange traded fund (IWM) by an average of 1.73% per year. That's a total annual return of 7.67% for the S&P Small Cap 600 versus 5.94% for the Russell 2000 Small Cap, paid by the respective funds or cumulatively 142.80% to 99.91% during that twelve year period. See Spreadsheets 2.3 and 2.4

If you take the two Small Cap indexes and go back to the early 1990s you will find the trend almost exactly the same. That's quite a difference for two exchange traded funds, or the indexes representing the same sector of the market. As always, past performance does not guarantee future results.

Another thing to keep in mind is, that small cap fund managers will most always compare themselves to the 'Russell 2000 Small Cap Index' instead of the 'S&P 600 Small Cap Index', because they know it is a *lower bar for them to climb.* Obviously, that makes it easier for them look good in your eyes. Of course, none of them are very likely to admit as much, but now you are better informed.

We will use the *total return* of all the stocks and ETFs when we calculate returns in the examples used in this book. This is the real return you could have made with your investment, because you can't invest directly in the indexes, only in a replica (such as an ETF or mutual fund) of the index.

Some of the mutual funds offered in some of the smaller employer plans do not even list a ticker symbol. If this is the case in your plan, you need to talk to your plan administrator and ask if the fund tracks another fund that does have a symbol and see what that symbol is. Then you should watch the fund very closely and see if does indeed mirror the index.

Spreadsheet 2.1

Mr, Ms Smart Investor

Pay Period	Gross Salary	Employee Cont Percent	Employee Cont Dollars	Company Match 3.00%
1	3,000	23.00%	690	90
2	3,000	23.00%	690	90
3	3,000	23.00%	690	90
4	3,000	23.00%	690	90
5	3,000	23.00%	690	90
6	3,000	23.00%	690	90
7	3,000	23.00%	690	90
8	3,000	23.00%	690	90
9	3,000	23.00%	690	90
10	3,000	23.00%	690	90
11	3,000	23.00%	690	90
12	3,000	23.00%	690	90
13	3,000	23.00%	690	90
14	3,000	23.00%	690	90
15	3,000	23.00%	690	90
16	3,000	23.00%	690	90
17	3,000	22.00%	660	90
18	3,000	22.00%	660	90
19	3,000	22.00%	660	90
20	3,000	22.00%	660	90
21	3,000	22.00%	660	90
22	3,000	22.00%	660	90
23	3,000	22.00%	660	90
24	3,000	22.00%	660	90
25	3,000	22.00%	660	90
26	3,000	17.32%	520	90
Total	78,000		17,500	2,340

Spreadsheet 2.2
Mr, Ms Not so Smart Investor

Pay Period	Gross Salary	Employee Cont Percent	Employee Cont Dollars	Company Match 3.00%
1	3,000	50.00%	1,500	90
2	3,000	50.00%	1,500	90
3	3,000	50.00%	1,500	90
4	3,000	50.00%	1,500	90
5	3,000	50.00%	1,500	90
6	3,000	50.00%	1,500	90
7	3,000	50.00%	1,500	90
8	3,000	50.00%	1,500	90
9	3,000	50.00%	1,500	90
10	3,000	50.00%	1,500	90
11	3,000	50.00%	1,500	90
12	3,000	33.33%	1,000	90
13	3,000		0	
14	3,000		0	
15	3,000		0	
16	3,000		0	
17	3,000		0	
18	3,000		0	
19	3,000		0	
20	3,000		0	
21	3,000		0	
22	3,000		0	
23	3,000		0	
24	3,000		0	
25	3,000		0	
26	3,000		0	
Total	78,000		17,500	1,080

Spreads 2.3 I Shares S & P 600 Small Cap IJR

Yr End 31-Dec	Begin Price	Div Amt Per Website	Div Pct	End Price	Gain Loss %	$ Value Cumlative	Yearly Ave Ret 7.67%		
2000						1,000	1,000		
2001	108.09	0.580	0.54%	114.40	6.37%	1,064	1,077		
2002	114.40	0.632	0.55%	97.45	-14.26%	912	1,159		
2003	97.45	0.815	0.84%	134.00	38.34%	1,262	1,248		
2004	134.00	1.193	0.89%	162.71	22.32%	1,543	1,344		
2005	54.24	0.502	0.93%	57.80	7.50%	1,659	1,447		
2006	57.80	0.490	0.85%	65.99	15.02%	1,908	1,558	As of 31-Dec-12	
2007	65.99	0.693	1.05%	65.02	-0.42%	1,900	1,678	Cumulative Tot	
2008	65.02	0.660	1.01%	43.97	-31.36%	1,304	1,806	48.15%	3 yrs
2009	43.97	0.535	1.22%	54.72	25.67%	1,639	1,945	27.79%	5 yrs
2010	54.72	0.735	1.34%	68.47	26.47%	2,073	2,094	57.33%	8 yrs
2011	68.47	0.700	1.02%	68.30	0.77%	2,089	2,255	166.23%	10 yrs
2012	68.30	1.293	1.89%	78.10	16.24%	2,428	2,428	142.80%	12 yrs

Spreads 2.4 I Shares Russell 2000 Small Cap IWM

Yr End 31-Dec	Begin Price	Div Amt Per Website	Div Pct	End Price	Gain Loss %	$ Value Cumlative	Yearly Ave Ret 5.94%		
2000						1,000	1,000		
2001	95.75	0.521	0.54%	96.35	1.17%	1,012	1,059		
2002	96.35	0.497	0.52%	75.81	-20.80%	801	1,122		
2003	75.81	0.461	0.61%	110.80	46.76%	1,176	1,189		
2004	110.80	0.595	0.54%	129.50	17.41%	1,381	1,260		
2005	64.75	0.742	1.15%	66.72	4.19%	1,439	1,334		
2006	66.72	0.834	1.25%	78.03	18.20%	1,700	1,414	As of 31-Dec-12	
2007	78.03	0.775	0.99%	75.90	-1.74%	1,671	1,498	Cumulative Tot	
2008	75.90	0.878	1.16%	49.24	-33.97%	1,103	1,587	41.26%	3 yrs
2009	49.24	0.720	1.46%	62.44	28.27%	1,415	1,681	19.65%	5 yrs
2010	62.44	0.893	1.43%	78.24	26.73%	1,794	1,781	44.79%	8 yrs
2011	78.24	1.031	1.32%	73.75	-4.42%	1,714	1,887	149.50%	10 yrs
2012	73.75	1.687	2.29%	84.32	16.62%	1,999	1,999	99.91%	12 yrs

CHAPTER THREE

MUTUAL FUNDS
WHY YOU SHOULDN'T INVEST IN THEM
(UNLESS YOU HAVE NO OTHER CHOICE)

Mutual funds, which also have been known as Investment Trusts, got their start in Europe during the 1700s. Of course they have been refined over the years, in some cases to benefit those whom sell and manage them. Over the years in modern times many U.S. based mutual funds have been merged or dissolved or had their name changed. This usually happens after a period of poor performance, which helps the mutual fund families to keep us confused. Mutual funds are only priced once per day after the market closes. In addition, options and futures can't be bought or sold based on their values.

Why Shouldn't You Invest In Mutual Funds?

Let Me Count a Few of the Ways.

1) Fees Are Usually Way too High.
According to the 'Securities and Exchange Commission' (SEC) website mutual funds can charge you a sales load up to 8.5%. That's just the sales load. That doesn't count the management fees that can add 2% or more per year, and now get this: what's known as 12b-1 fees. The theory being that 12b-1 fees are for advertising, supposedly that attracting more investors in these funds benefits current investors. What a farce, only a mutual fund company manager or their lobbyists could think such an idea could be good. Here is a better idea: Lower fees and better performance

will attract more investors. Of course, this is not likely to happen since in most cases the big mutual fund companies have a captive audience in their employer plans. The average yearly expense in a mutual fund is over 1% per year. The average ETF fund charges about 50 basis points in expenses per year. (100 basis points is equal to 1%).

Many index funds including mutual funds offered by Vanguard are no load funds with a very low (some less than 0.1%) annual fees. Look for these to invest in your 401k/403b if your plan only offers mutual funds. Most plans offer a fund that tracks the S&P 500 Index.

2) Not So Professional Management

According to a recent article in a leading financial publication only two of the ten biggest mutual fund families posted a positive return for 2011. Collectively, the funds posted a negative 1% return for 2011. Remember, the two largest S&P 500 ETF funds (ticker symbols SPY & IVV) posted an average 1.84% total return for 2011. That's almost a 3% difference in performance. Throughout the years this has been a very typical comparison. Mutual fund managers have been known to use sneaky tricks to make you think they have great expertise. Example: take a large cap balanced fund and invest 80-90% of the fund in the S&P 500 Index. Then take the balance and invest in whatever the hot money is in (also known as following the herd). If the hot money part performs well, then the manager is a genius and you will hear a lot of bragging. If it doesn't, he still hasn't underperformed by enough to be in hot water and the fund managers hope you don't notice.

3) Very High Turnover Rates in Most Funds.

Many mutual funds have an average turnover in excess of 100% per year. This would mean on average each stock in the fund would be sold once each year. In my personal portfolios, my turnover was about 29% in 2011. It could have been much lower if I weren't retired and needed to raise some cash for living expenses. The more a mutual fund manager can buy and sell in the fund—the more he makes in transaction fees for his brokerage company to be paid out of your mutual fund.

4) Taxes

Mutual funds are also required to pay taxes on their capital gains on each trade each year even if the fund loses money. Whether you have a mutual fund in a taxable account, or in a tax advantaged account the fund will still pay taxes on its capital gains. An ETF does not have this problem because ETFs are structured differently. Most mutual funds are structured as pools of assets and each investor shares in the pool. When more money comes into the mutual fund company, it buys up more shares of stock and must sell the shares of stock when sell orders come in. Most ETFs don't have this pooling feature. When you buy an ETF, you are just purchasing a group of stocks from another investor, and no shares of the securities in the ETF are actually sold. This is considered an 'in-kind' exchange that is not a taxable event.

5) The Lipper Mutual Fund Averages

The fact that a certain family of mutual funds beat their Lipper Mutual Fund averages is not much to brag about. It's like becoming the Minor League champion of your favorite sport, and comparing those statistics to the Major League guys. Take a look at how 'large cap blend funds' compare to the S&P 500 ETFs (SPY or IVV) for a three year period. Do the same with the 'mid cap blend funds' to the S&P 400 Mid Cap ETF (IJH), and 'small cap blend funds' to the S&P 600 Small Cap ETF (IJR). In most cases the ETF index funds (with much lower fees) will win out.

6) Salesmanship

The problem from our perspective on mutual funds is that the big companies put much more emphasis in training sales people than they do in finding better returns. They will only tell you what they want you to know, not what you should know. They do this by working (conspiring) with your employers to set up these 401k/403b plans, to give you limited choices in just a few mutual funds with high fees in many cases. This is how the big mutual fund companies make a lot of money, and at the same time your employer can pass the blame on to someone else.

7) Name of Mutual Fund Can Be Deceiving

Today, there are about 7,600 mutual funds available in the United States with about $11 trillion in assets under management according to Zacks.com. In the past many mutual funds have reinvented themselves without changing their name. For example a small cap value fund could start performing very well. Isn't that good news? Yes, if you got into the fund early and profited as the fund does well in the early years. But now your natural reaction is you tell your friends and neighbors about this great fund you are in. Then, they all say I want a piece of this action and they send their money in. With all this new money coming in the fund managers basically have several choices:

- Invest is less attractive small cap stocks
- Invest in mid cap or even large cap stocks
- Close the fund to new investors

The last option would probably be the best for investors in the fund. It is also the least likely choice that would be made. Empire building, with a very few exceptions, is just too tempting for most mutual fund companies to walk away from.

8) Disclosure Requirements

Another big difference between mutual funds and ETFs is the underlying holdings of the funds, and how often the information is released. ETFs are required to release on a daily basis what their portfolio of securities is made up of, and the size of their positions in the fund. This allows investors to find out what trades have been made and when they were made.

However, mutual funds are only required to disclose their positions on a quarterly basis. As you can see, this allows all sorts of changes and moves that allows the manager to rapidly trade just before the disclosure date. The mutual fund investor is not going to know if an issue was bought and sold between disclosure dates, but you should be very suspicious when you see 80% and higher turnover rates in a given year.

9) No Intra-Day Trading

The biggest single difference between ETFs and mutual funds that you will notice is the way they're traded. No matter what time of the day you put in your order to buy or sell your mutual fund shares, it will only be traded at the end of the day at the net asset value (NAV) of all the securities in the fund. If you miss the cutoff time your buy or sell order must wait until the closing of the next trading day. On the other hand ETF investors do not face any of the above restrictions. They can buy or sell, (or both buy and sell) throughout the trading day just like a stock. You can also buy and sell options on ETFs.

10) Do Nothing Boards of Directors

Yes, believe it or not, mutual funds have 'Boards of Directors'. They are required to by law. (The funds no doubt lobbied for these laws) They are supposed to be looking out for investors, but that is not always the case. For instance, forty percent of the board is required to be independent, but so called independent directors can be former executives of the same fund. These **independent directors**, by themselves decide what their pay should be. At the largest funds the average pay for directors is about $260,000 per year. Not bad pay for a part time job if you can get it. This is, of course, paid out of the expense that the shareholders are charged. Exchange Traded Funds (ETFs) are the much preferred alternative, even though there are only about 1,400 total ETF funds with a grand total of about $1 trillion in assets under management.

As you can see the bottom line on mutual funds is just don't own them unless you don't have any other choice in your 401k/403b. There are naysayers out there that will tell you to look at this or that mutual fund, but you don't want to waste your time looking for that proverbial needle in a haystack. You are most likely a working person that needs to manage your time between, work, family, and maybe school, and oh yeah, a little fun time too. You can better manage that time spent on managing your investments by ignoring a group of underperformers like mutual funds. If you were to buy and hold forever an S&P 500 ETF such as (ticker symbols) SPY or IVV you would very likely out perform at least 2/3 of the mutual fund managers over the long term. (Ticker symbol 'IVV' stands for the I-Shares S&P 500 Index ETF which is comparable to SPY)

With all the talk in Washington, DC about wanting lower taxes, the financial services industry could show good faith by doing away with mutual funds and convert them to ETFs. In all probability, this will be a slow process at best. We can all help this process along by becoming better informed investors.

CHAPTER FOUR
THE BUSINESS CYCLE

In order to be a successful investor you need to understand the business cycle. You also need to focus on the long term trends more than short term gyrations. One way to understand this is to take the S&P 500 Index SPDR fund (SPY) and divide it into nine different ETFs which by the way you can purchase individually.

Please take a look at the list with their ticker symbols, and the percentage of the S&P 500 that each sector represents on Spreadsheet 4.1. This is the percentage exposure you would have in each sector if you bought *one* exchange traded fund (SPY). In addition, if you were to buy an S&P 500 Index mutual fund you should get approximately the same exposure to each sector. Keep in mind that these percentages will probably change a little by the time you read this. The latest information can be found at www.sectorspdr.com.

We will refer to the sector funds listed in Spreadsheet 4.1 as 'The SPDR Nine'. Sometimes in the financial press you will hear references to the *ten* Sectors of the S&P 500. The only difference in this case is the taking of the telecommunication companies from the technology sector and making the S&P 500 into ten sectors. With nine sectors they are both included in the technology sector ETF (XLK). This also explains the major difference in performance between the XLK and the NASDAQ 100 Index.

If you were to buy each of 'The SPDR Nine' ETFs separately in equal dollar amounts you would have 11.1% invested in each sector of the S&P 500 and *not* the percentages listed in Spreadsheet 4.1. When you look at the total performance for the three, five, nine, ten and fourteen year performance on Spreadsheet 4.2 you can see that equally weighted 'The SPDR Nine' has outperformed the SPY and DIA index ETFs over different time periods. The Rydex Equal Weight S&P 500 (ticker RSP) comparison is also included in Spreadsheet 4.2. The RSP wasn't created until 2003, so we only have a nine calendar year performance to include. You can see that the ETF for the Dow Industrials (DIA) does come closer in performance, but it is only thirty stocks and as previously discussed it tends to be a little more volatile in comparison. Investing in the SPDR Nine or the 'SPY' would give you broader diversification.

Why has the equal weighted 'SPDR Nine' outperformed the S&P 500 in recent years? Let's take a look at four of the nine ETF sectors. The Financial (XLF) with 15.61% and the Technology (XLK) with 22.10% are the two sectors with highest percentage of the S&P 500 index, and are also the only two sectors with a flat or negative return. They are also the only sectors to underperform the S&P 500 (SPY) over this fourteen year period. (See Spreadsheets 4.3-4.11) If you had only owned them in equal sector dollar amounts you would not be as much exposed as you would in the capitalization weighted SPY as summarized in Spreadsheet 4.2. At the other end of the spectrum are the Utilities (XLU) and the Materials (XLB) sectors. With each at only about 3.43% and 3.62% respectfully, of the S&P 500 their good or bad performance does not have much of an impact on the whole index. If you owned the 'SPDR Nine' in equal dollar amounts you would have 11.1% in each of the Materials (XLB) and the Utilities (XLU) sectors. Over the last fourteen years utilities have always been the 'Steady Eddies' of the stock market and probably will continue to be for our lifetimes to come. You should keep at least 10% of your portfolio in the Utility Sector at all times.

If we go back to the 1990s the opposite was true. If you had invested heavily in technology, you would have outperformed the market. This brings another cliché to mind. *"In the long term it all reverts to the mean."* This means that a period of outperformance will usually be followed by a period of underperformance, and vice versa. The party will most always come to an end. There was one source in the financial press in the late 1990s that predicted the NASDAQ Composite Index would soon go to 25,000. As you probably know, it topped out at a little over 5,000 and soon fell to 1,108 in 2002.

The lesson here is no matter how high the market goes, it will not be as high as at least one overly optimistic prediction that you will hear in the financial press. At the other end the opposite is also true. When the market is at the very bottom, some gloom and doom 'expert' will predict the market will fall much more.

The business cycle has three phases. Let's look at which S&P 500 Index ETF sector funds usually do best in each phase of the business cycle:

First let's take the *defensive* cycle, which usually does best in a bear (down) market. The sector ETFs that usually do best would be:

XLP -- Consumer Staples
XLV -- Health Care
XLU – Utilities

The defensive portion of 'The SPDR Nine' is approximately 26.05% of the S&P 500 market cap as we go to press.

Next would be the *recovery* cycle, which usually does best when we first come out of a recession. The sector ETFs that usually do best would be:

XLY -- Consumer Discretionary
XLF -- Financials
XLK – Technology

The Recovery portion of 'The SPDR Nine' is approximately 49.21% of the S&P 500 market cap as we go to press.

This should also be noted: Small cap stocks ETFs like the S&P 600 (IJR) and the Russell 2000 (IWM) will also usually do well coming out of a recession, but keep in mind these are not part of 'The SPDR Nine' or the S&P 500 Index. Remember what was discussed in Chapter Two. When investing in small caps the S&P 600 Index usually (but not always) out performs the Russell 2000 Index over the long term.

Next would be the *final* cycle. You'll know were in this phase when the politicians in power start taking all the credit for the good times, and want you to believe that if you re-elect them the good times will never end. Of course, this has never happened and probably never will. The sector ETFs that usually do the best in this cycle are:

XLE -- Energy
XLI -- Industrials
XLB – Materials

The Final portion of 'The SPDR Nine' is approximately 24.73% of the S&P 500 market cap as we go to press.

See Spreadsheets 4.3 through 4.12 for a summation of how the above mentioned 'SPDR Nine' sector ETFs as well as the three business cycle groups, have preformed from January 1999 through December 2012 (fourteen years). Of course no two business cycles are exactly alike. For the first time in the last twelve years the Financial sector (XLF) was the leading sector of the 'SPDR Nine' in the 2012 calendar year. You should keep at least 5% but not more than 20% of your portfolio in dividend payers from each sector of the S&P 500. This will keep you well diversified and keep portfolio damage to a minimum in case we have another meltdown like tech stocks in the early 2000s or the more recent financial meltdown.

Spreadsheet 4.1	Business Cycle				
SPDR Nine Sector Funds	Trading Symbol	Percent S&P 500	Defensive Cycle	Recovery Cycle	Final Cycle
Consumer Staples	X L P	10.61%	10.61%		
Health Care	X L V	12.01%	12.01%		
Utilities	X L U	3.43%	3.43%		
Consumer Discretionary	X L Y	11.50%		11.50%	
Financial	X L F	15.61%		15.61%	
Technology (Including Telecom)	X L K	22.10%		22.10%	
Energy	X L E	10.99%			10.99%
Industrial	X L I	10.12%			10.12%
Materials	X L B	3.62%			3.62%
Total		99.99%	26.05%	49.21%	24.73%

Spreads 4.2 Yr End 31-Dec	% Total Return SPY	$ Value 1,000 SPY	% Total Return SPDR Nine = wt	$ Value 1,000	% Total Return DIA	$ Value 1,000 DIA	% Total Return RSP	$ Value 1,000 RSP
1999	20.26%	1,203	17.17%	1,172	27.74%	1,277		
2000	-9.69%	1,086	1.95%	1,195	-5.94%	1,202		
2001	-12.09%	955	-7.80%	1,101	-5.08%	1,141		
2002	-21.50%	749	-18.31%	900	-13.78%	983		
2003	27.97%	959	28.00%	1,152	27.53%	1,254		
2004	10.59%	1,061	14.10%	1,314	4.92%	1,316	16.38%	1,164
2005	4.79%	1,111	7.95%	1,418	1.56%	1,336	7.37%	1,250
2006	15.47%	1,283	15.48%	1,638	18.69%	1,586	15.38%	1,442
2007	5.15%	1,350	10.29%	1,806	8.75%	1,725	0.95%	1,456
2008	-36.42%	858	-35.05%	1,173	-32.33%	1,167	-39.71%	878
2009	26.05%	1,082	26.98%	1,490	22.05%	1,425	44.08%	1,264
2010	14.84%	1,242	15.72%	1,724	12.98%	1,610	21.19%	1,532
2011	1.85%	1,265	3.07%	1,777	7.95%	1,737	-0.66%	1,522
2012	15.95%	1,467	14.54%	2,035	9.88%	1,909	17.10%	1,782
3 years cumulative	35.62%		36.60%		34.01%		40.97%	
5 years cumulative	8.69%		12.67%		10.67%		22.46%	
9 years cumulative	52.93%		76.74%		52.22%		78.25%	
10 years cumulative	95.71%		126.23%		94.13%			
14 years cumulative	46.68%		103.53%		90.91%			

Spreads 4.3 Yr End 31-Dec	SPDR Consumer Stpl			Defense Cycle		X L P	Yearly		
	Begin Price	Div Amt Per	Div Pct	End Price	Gain Loss %	$Value Cumul	Ave Return 3.90%		
1998		Website				1,000	1,000		
1999	27.03	0.27	1.00%	23.03	-13.80%	862	1,039		
2000	23.03	0.30	1.30%	28.56	25.31%	1,080	1,079		
2001	28.56	0.32	1.12%	25.40	-9.94%	973	1,122		
2002	25.40	0.38	1.51%	19.94	-19.98%	778	1,165		
2003	19.94	0.37	1.86%	21.78	11.08%	865	1,211		
2004	21.78	0.36	1.64%	23.16	7.98%	934	1,258		
2005	23.16	0.44	1.91%	23.31	2.56%	957	1,307		
2006	23.31	0.51	2.18%	26.12	14.23%	1,094	1,358		
2007	26.12	0.57	2.18%	28.80	12.44%	1,230	1,411		
2008	28.80	0.64	2.22%	23.87	-14.90%	1,047	1,466	As of 31-Dec-12	
2009	23.87	0.73	3.05%	26.47	13.94%	1,193	1,523	Cumulative Tot	
2010	26.47	0.76	2.88%	29.31	13.61%	1,355	1,582	38.87%	5 yrs
2011	29.31	0.89	3.02%	32.49	13.87%	1,543	1,644	119.42%	10 yrs
2012	32.49	1.07	3.28%	34.90	10.70%	1,708	1,708	70.79%	14 yrs

Spread 4.4 Yr End 31-Dec	SPDR Healthcare			Defensive Cycle		X L V	Yearly		
	Begin Price	Div Amt Per	Div Pct	End Price	Gain Loss %	$Value Cumul	Ave Return 4.42%		
1998		Website				1,000	1,000		
1999	26.00	0.18	0.68%	30.89	19.48%	1,195	1,044		
2000	30.89	0.06	0.19%	27.25	-11.59%	1,056	1,090		
2001	27.25	0.07	0.26%	26.95	-0.84%	1,047	1,139		
2002	26.95	0.20	0.73%	26.55	-0.75%	1,040	1,189		
2003	26.55	0.35	1.31%	30.15	14.87%	1,194	1,242		
2004	30.15	0.34	1.14%	30.19	1.27%	1,209	1,296		
2005	30.19	0.39	1.29%	31.73	6.39%	1,287	1,354		
2006	31.73	0.44	1.39%	33.49	6.94%	1,376	1,414		
2007	33.49	0.56	1.67%	35.31	7.11%	1,474	1,476		
2008	35.31	0.56	1.59%	26.55	-23.22%	1,131	1,541	As of 31-Dec-12	
2009	26.55	0.57	2.16%	31.07	19.19%	1,349	1,610	Cumulative Tot	
2010	31.07	0.58	1.86%	31.50	3.24%	1,392	1,681	24.41%	5 yrs
2011	31.50	0.68	2.16%	34.69	12.29%	1,563	1,755	76.36%	10 yrs
2012	34.69	0.80	2.31%	39.88	17.27%	1,833	1,833	83.34%	14 yrs

Spread 4.5 Yr End 31-Dec	SPDR Utilities Defensive Cycle				X L U	Yearly Ave		
	Begin Price	Div Amt Per Website	Div Pct	End Price	Gain Loss %	$Value Cumul	Return 4.68%	
1998						1,000	1,000	
1999	30.23	0.96	3.18%	28.14	-3.74%	963	1,047	
2000	28.14	1.16	4.12%	33.19	22.07%	1,175	1,096	
2001	33.19	0.88	2.65%	28.03	-12.90%	1,024	1,147	
2002	28.03	0.92	3.28%	19.15	-28.40%	733	1,201	
2003	19.15	0.80	4.16%	23.33	25.99%	923	1,257	
2004	23.33	0.87	3.75%	27.85	23.12%	1,137	1,315	
2005	27.85	1.01	3.63%	31.39	16.34%	1,323	1,377	
2006	31.39	1.11	3.54%	36.72	20.52%	1,594	1,441	
2007	36.72	1.07	2.91%	42.33	18.19%	1,884	1,509	
2008	42.33	1.22	2.88%	29.03	-28.54%	1,346	1,579	As of 31-Dec-12
2009	29.03	1.27	4.39%	31.02	11.24%	1,498	1,653	Cumulative Tot
2010	31.02	1.27	4.10%	31.34	5.13%	1,574	1,730	0.66% 5 yrs
2011	31.34	1.37	4.37%	35.98	19.17%	1,876	1,811	158.75% 10 yrs
2012	35.98	1.45	4.02%	34.92	1.07%	1,896	1,896	89.63% 14 yrs

Spread 4.6 Yr End 31-Dec	SPDR Consumer Disc Recovery Cycle				X L Y	Yearly Ave		
	Begin Price	Div Amt Per Website	Div Pct	End Price	Gain Loss %	$Value Cumul	Return 5.48%	
1998						1,000	1,000	
1999	26.12	0.15	0.57%	31.06	19.49%	1,195	1,055	
2000	31.06	0.23	0.74%	25.59	-16.87%	993	1,113	
2001	25.59	0.22	0.86%	28.60	12.62%	1,119	1,174	
2002	28.60	0.17	0.60%	23.11	-18.60%	911	1,238	
2003	23.11	0.19	0.82%	31.49	37.08%	1,248	1,306	
2004	31.49	0.24	0.76%	35.42	13.24%	1,414	1,377	
2005	35.42	0.33	0.92%	32.63	-6.95%	1,315	1,453	
2006	32.63	0.27	0.83%	38.36	18.39%	1,557	1,532	
2007	38.36	0.43	1.12%	32.70	-13.63%	1,345	1,616	
2008	32.70	0.41	1.25%	21.57	-32.78%	904	1,705	As of 31-Dec-12
2009	21.57	0.45	2.09%	29.77	40.11%	1,266	1,798	Cumulative Tot
2010	29.77	0.49	1.65%	37.41	27.32%	1,612	1,897	56.89% 5 yrs
2011	37.41	0.61	1.62%	39.02	5.93%	1,708	2,001	131.69% 10 yrs
2012	39.02	0.76	1.95%	47.44	23.53%	2,110	2,110	110.98% 14 yrs

Spread 4.7 Yr End 31-Dec	SPDR Financial			Recovery Cycle		X L F	Yearly Ave Return		
	Begin Price	Div Amt Per	Div Pct	End Price	Gain Loss %	$Value Cumul	-0.46%		
1998		Website				1,000	1,000		
1999	23.44	0.30	1.28%	23.77	2.69%	1,027	995		
2000	23.77	0.36	1.51%	29.50	25.62%	1,290	991		
2001	29.50	0.40	1.36%	26.30	-9.49%	1,168	986		
2002	26.30	0.45	1.71%	22.00	-14.64%	997	982		
2003	22.00	0.52	2.34%	28.13	30.20%	1,298	977		
2004	28.13	0.63	2.22%	30.53	10.75%	1,437	973		
2005	30.53	0.71	2.33%	31.67	6.06%	1,524	968		
2006	31.67	0.84	2.65%	36.74	18.66%	1,809	964		
2007	36.74	0.85	2.31%	28.93	-18.94%	1,466	959		
2008	28.93	0.76	2.63%	12.52	-54.10%	673	955	As of 31-Dec-12	
2009	12.52	0.25	1.97%	14.40	16.98%	787	951	Cumulative Tot	
2010	14.40	0.16	1.09%	15.95	11.85%	881	946	-36.11%	5 yrs
2011	15.95	0.23	1.41%	13.00	-17.08%	730	942	-6.01%	10 yrs
2012	13.00	0.29	2.21%	16.39	28.29%	937	937	-6.33%	14 yrs

Spread 4.8 Yr End 31-Dec	SPDR Technology			Recovery Cycle		X L K	Yearly Ave Return		
	Begin Price	Div Amt Per	Div Pct	End Price	Gain Loss %	$Value Cumul	0.00%		
1998		Website				1,000	1,000		
1999	32.62	0.00	0.00%	53.88	65.18%	1,652	1,000		
2000	53.88	0.00	0.00%	31.31	-41.89%	960	1,000		
2001	31.31	0.00	0.00%	24.00	-23.34%	736	1,000		
2002	24.00	0.04	0.17%	14.80	-38.16%	455	1,000		
2003	14.80	0.14	0.95%	20.38	38.66%	631	1,000		
2004	20.38	0.42	2.06%	21.11	5.64%	666	1,000		
2005	21.11	0.15	0.70%	20.90	-0.29%	665	1,000		
2006	20.90	0.17	0.81%	23.26	12.11%	745	1,000		
2007	23.26	0.18	0.77%	26.66	15.39%	860	1,000		
2008	26.66	0.21	0.79%	15.41	-41.41%	504	1,000	As of 31-Dec-12	
2009	15.41	0.31	2.04%	22.93	50.84%	760	1,000	Cumulative Tot	
2010	22.93	0.32	1.41%	25.19	11.26%	845	1,000	16.31%	5 yrs
2011	25.19	0.38	1.53%	25.45	2.56%	867	1,000	119.74%	10 yrs
2012	25.45	0.50	1.97%	28.85	15.33%	1,000	1,000	-0.02%	14 yrs

Spread 4.9 Yr End 31-Dec	SPDR Energy Begin Price	Div Amt Per	Div Pct	Final Cycle End Price	Gain Loss %	X L E $Value Cumul	Yearly Ave Return 10.07%	
1998		Website				1,000	1,000	
1999	23.19	0.45	1.94%	27.09	18.76%	1,188	1,101	
2000	27.09	0.48	1.77%	33.19	24.29%	1,476	1,211	
2001	33.19	0.49	1.48%	26.70	-18.08%	1,209	1,333	
2002	26.70	0.48	1.81%	22.33	-14.56%	1,033	1,468	
2003	22.33	0.48	2.15%	27.55	25.53%	1,297	1,615	
2004	27.55	0.51	1.85%	36.23	33.36%	1,729	1,778	
2005	36.23	0.57	1.57%	50.26	40.30%	2,426	1,957	
2006	50.26	0.71	1.41%	58.63	18.07%	2,865	2,154	
2007	58.63	0.76	1.30%	79.35	36.64%	3,914	2,371	
2008	79.35	0.86	1.08%	47.77	-38.71%	2,399	2,610	As of 31-Dec-12
2009	47.77	1.03	2.16%	57.01	21.51%	2,915	2,872	Cumulative Tot
2010	57.01	1.00	1.75%	68.25	21.46%	3,541	3,161	-2.15% 5 yrs
2011	68.25	1.06	1.56%	69.13	2.84%	3,641	3,480	270.76% 10 yrs
2012	69.13	1.30	1.88%	71.42	5.19%	3,830	3,830	283.04% 14 yrs

Spread 4.10 Yr End 31-Dec	SPDR Industrials Begin Price	Div Amt Per	Div Pct	Final Cycle End Price	Gain Loss %	X L I $Value Cumul	Yearly Ave Return 5.01%	
1998		Website				1,000	1,000	
1999	24.31	0.38	1.56%	29.61	23.36%	1,234	1,050	
2000	29.61	0.33	1.11%	31.25	6.65%	1,316	1,103	
2001	31.25	0.34	1.09%	27.70	-10.27%	1,181	1,158	
2002	27.70	0.33	1.19%	20.59	-24.47%	892	1,216	
2003	20.59	0.34	1.67%	26.76	31.63%	1,174	1,277	
2004	26.76	0.40	1.51%	31.18	18.03%	1,385	1,340	
2005	31.18	0.49	1.57%	31.73	3.34%	1,431	1,408	
2006	31.73	0.63	1.99%	35.01	12.32%	1,608	1,478	
2007	35.01	0.55	1.57%	39.16	13.42%	1,824	1,552	
2008	39.16	0.76	1.94%	23.42	-38.25%	1,126	1,630	As of 31-Dec-12
2009	23.42	0.65	2.76%	27.79	21.42%	1,367	1,711	Cumulative Tot
2010	27.79	0.59	2.11%	34.87	27.59%	1,744	1,797	8.61% 5 yrs
2011	34.87	0.73	2.09%	33.75	-1.13%	1,725	1,887	122.15% 10 yrs
2012	33.75	0.86	2.55%	37.90	14.84%	1,981	1,981	98.08% 14 yrs

Spread 4.11 Yr End 31-Dec	SPDR Materials Begin Price	Div Amt Per Website	Div Pct	Final Cycle End Price	Gain Loss %	X L B $ Value Cumul	Yearly Ave Return 6.37%		
1998						1,000	1,000		
1999	21.92	0.400	1.82%	26.58	23.08%	1,231	1,064		
2000	26.58	0.900	3.39%	21.42	-16.03%	1,034	1,131		
2001	21.42	0.440	2.05%	21.42	2.05%	1,055	1,204		
2002	21.42	0.454	2.12%	19.84	-5.26%	999	1,280		
2003	19.84	0.478	2.41%	26.69	36.94%	1,368	1,362		
2004	26.69	0.506	1.90%	29.79	13.51%	1,553	1,448		
2005	29.79	0.635	2.13%	30.28	3.78%	1,612	1,541		
2006	30.28	0.930	3.07%	34.84	18.13%	1,904	1,639		
2007	34.84	0.800	2.30%	41.70	21.99%	2,323	1,743		
2008	41.70	0.810	1.94%	22.74	-43.53%	1,312	1,854	As of 31-Dec-12	
2009	22.74	0.579	2.55%	32.99	47.62%	1,937	1,972	Cumulative Tot	
2010	32.99	1.178	3.57%	38.41	20.00%	2,324	2,098	2.20%	5 yrs
2011	38.41	0.737	1.92%	33.50	-10.86%	2,072	2,232	137.56%	10 yrs
2012	33.50	0.853	2.55%	37.54	14.61%	2,374	2,374	137.41%	14 yrs

Total Returns Spreadsheet 4.12		Cal Year 1999	Cal Year 2000	Cal Year 2001	Cal Year 2002	Cal Year 2003	Cal Year 2004	Cal Year 2005	Cal Year 2006	Cal Year 2007	Cal Year 2008	Cal Year 2009	Cal Year 2010	Cal Year 2011	Cal Year 2012
Defensive Cycle															
Consumer Stpl	XLP	-13.80%	25.31%	-9.94%	-19.98%	11.08%	7.98%	2.56%	14.23%	12.44%	-14.90%	13.94%	13.61%	13.87%	10.70%
Healthcare	XLV	19.48%	-11.59%	-0.84%	-0.75%	14.87%	1.27%	6.39%	6.94%	7.11%	-23.22%	19.19%	3.24%	12.29%	17.27%
Utilities	XLU	-3.74%	22.07%	-12.90%	-28.40%	25.99%	23.12%	16.34%	20.52%	18.19%	-28.54%	11.24%	5.13%	19.17%	1.07%
Defensive Cycle Ave		0.65%	11.93%	-7.89%	-16.38%	17.31%	10.79%	8.43%	13.90%	12.58%	-22.22%	14.79%	7.33%	15.11%	9.68%
Recovery Cycle															
Consumer Disc	XLY	19.49%	-16.87%	12.62%	-18.60%	37.08%	13.24%	-6.95%	18.39%	-13.63%	-32.78%	40.11%	27.32%	5.93%	23.53%
Financial	XLF	2.69%	25.62%	-9.49%	-14.64%	30.20%	10.75%	6.06%	18.66%	-18.94%	-54.10%	16.98%	11.85%	-17.08%	28.29%
Technology	XLK	65.18%	-41.89%	-23.34%	-38.16%	38.66%	5.64%	-0.29%	12.11%	15.39%	-41.41%	50.84%	11.26%	2.56%	15.33%
Recovery Cycle Ave		29.12%	-11.05%	-6.74%	-23.80%	35.31%	9.88%	-0.39%	16.39%	-5.73%	-42.76%	35.98%	16.81%	-2.86%	22.38%
Final Cycle															
Energy	XLE	18.76%	24.29%	-18.08%	-14.56%	25.53%	33.36%	40.30%	18.07%	36.64%	-38.71%	21.51%	21.46%	2.84%	5.19%
Industrials	XLI	23.36%	6.65%	-10.27%	-24.47%	31.63%	18.03%	3.34%	12.32%	13.42%	-38.25%	21.42%	27.59%	-1.13%	14.84%
Materials	XLB	23.08%	-16.03%	2.05%	-5.26%	36.94%	13.51%	3.78%	18.13%	21.99%	-43.53%	47.62%	20.00%	-10.86%	14.61%
Final Cycle Average		21.73%	4.97%	-8.77%	-14.76%	31.37%	21.63%	15.81%	16.17%	24.02%	-40.16%	30.18%	23.02%	-3.05%	11.55%

Investing Made Easy

CHAPTER FIVE
BEAT THE MARKET WITH EXCHANGE TRADED FUNDS

The first modern Exchange Traded Fund (ETF) was the 'SPDR' (pronounced spider) S&P 500 Index (Ticker, SPY) which started trading January 22, 1993. As we go to press their expense is only 0.09% per year and the annual holdings turnover rate is only 3.72% per year. Options and futures can be bought and sold on ETFs, but not on mutual funds.

Today, there are over 1,400 ETFs available for trade each market trading day and the number seems to keep growing. Most of them track an index even though some of these indexes even the most knowledgeable investor never heard of, and were invented by the ones who created the ETF fund. There are a few crazy ones out there, and to quote a cliché that I strongly believe in: ***don't invest in something you don't understand, and be very skeptical if someone wants to teach you so you will do business with them. It's highly unlikely they will teach you what you SHOULD know, just what they want you to know.*** Whether you are investing in a mutual fund (if you have no other choice), or an ETF you should buy one with at least $1 Billion in net assets. Any fund with a lower amount is a candidate for higher than normal fees, merging, or closing with extra fees taken from *you*.

For example, Scottrade recently announced it was exiting the ETF business and will be liquidating its fifteen 'FocusShares' ETFs, which had just about $100 million in assets. Russell Investments also recently announced it was laying off thirty people. Russell's twenty-five ETFs only have a little over $300 million in assets. It's likely they will close most if not all of their ETFs. It looks like the ETF industry is beginning to consolidate among the big dogs of the industry. It doesn't appear that the ETF industry has peaked yet. Getting to an all ETF process and doing away with mutual funds will be a slow process at best. I do pray that we all live long enough to see it. The mutual fund companies don't want to give up their stranglehold on the captive 401k/403b industry that they now enjoy.

If your employer plan allows you to buy ETFs and stocks, you have one of the better plans and it makes your job of beating the market much easier. ETFs, on average have a much lower expense ratio and they usually track their indexes more closely. As you probably already know, the S&P 500 Index has been the standard by which the U.S. market has been measured since its creation in 1957. The Dow Jones Industrial Average (DJIA) is probably the most popular index in existence. The S&P 500 best represents how the market is performing even though the Dow has had a higher rate of return in recent years. There are two different things to keep in mind here. One is representing how the overall market is performing, and the other is which index is bringing the highest return. Don't forget to include dividends in your calculations, especially when measuring long term performance. This is what gives you your total return.

Back in the 1960s and 1970s the Dow Jones Industrial Average underperformed the S&P 500. This proves the point that the Dow is only thirty stocks and if one or two of them either outperforms or underperforms it will give a slightly inaccurate read on the entire market. If you want to go back to the early 1970s, and measure forward to today these two indexes have almost exactly the same performance over the longer time frame. There are several ways we can use these indexes to outperform the S&P 500. Let's look at how a few selected ETFs have performed over the last few years.

Let's remember that the S&P 500 Index is a capitalization weighted index. This means for example that Apple (AAPL) is about 4.32% of the S&P 500 Index as we go to press where as Proctor & Gamble (PG) is only about 1.51% based on their respective market capitalization. Market capitalization is the number of stock shares outstanding multiplied by the common stock price. The S&P 500 Exchange Traded Fund Symbol: (SPY) is the fund we will use as examples in this book, even though there are other excellent S&P 500 Index ETF funds.

Rydex Equal Weight 500, ETF Symbol (RSP): This exchange traded fund is not as well known, but it takes the S&P 500 Index and gives equal weight to each stock in the index. In this fund both Apple and Proctor & Gamble would have only 0.20% weights each, (1/500) in the fund.

The Dow Jones Industrial Average ETF Symbol (DIA): Is a price weighted index and to compensate for the effects of stock splits is now a scaled average. The value of the Dow is a sum of the component prices divided by a divisor that changes whenever there is a split in one of the components stock prices, or when stocks in the index changes. You can see the last fourteen full calendar year performances of the SPY and DIA index ETFs on Spreadsheets 5.1and 5.2 respectfully and the nine year performance on the Rydex (RSP) Equal Weight Index on Spreadsheet 5.3.

The S&P 600 Small Cap Index (IJR), and the Russell 2000 Small Cap Index (IWM), are both capitalization weighted indexes. You can see the last twelve calendar year performances of the above Small Cap index ETFs on Spreadsheets 2.3 and 2.4.

Listed below are the ETFs that you should follow closely, and are listed with their expense and turnover rates. You should become very familiar with these ticker symbols to take full advantage of what this book is all about. These are ETFs that you can invest in directly along with their index covered, and their expense and turnover percentages per year. You are encouraged to compare expense and turnover ratios to traditional mutual funds. Remember, the more turnover the higher the expenses are and the more the mutual fund is taxed which hurts returns whether you are in a taxable or tax advantaged account.

ETF Symbol	Index	Expense	Turnover
DIA	Dow Jones Industrial Ave	0.17%	5.52%
RSP	Guggenheim (Rydex) Equal Weight S&P 500	0.40%	20.00%
SPY	S & P 500	0.09%	3.80%
IJR	S & P 600 Small Cap	0.20%	18.00%
IWM	Russell 2000 Small Cap	0.20%	21.00%

	The SPDR Nine Sector Funds		
X L Y	S & P Consumer Disc	0.18%	4.80%
X L P	S & P Consumer Staples	0.18%	12.41%
X L E	S & P Energy	0.18%	5.47%
X L F	S & P Financial	0.18%	7.69%
X L I	S & P Industrial	0.18%	7.63%
X L B	S & P Materials	0.18%	11.58%
X L K	S & P Technology	0.18%	5.28%
X L V	S & P Health Care	0.18%	4.70%
X L U	S & P Utilities	0.18%	4.23%

As you can see the above ETFs have a lower expense ratio as well as a much lower turnover ratio. These ratios will compare favorably to most (at least 80%) of the mutual funds on the market today.

Keep in mind, the Dow Jones Industrial Average (DJIA) has only changed forty-nine times since 1896. That's an average of only once every 2+ years. If you choose to invest in the Dow Diamonds ETF (DIA), in many years you will experience a zero turnover rate. When it does change it usually makes the financial headlines. On the other hand, the S&P 500 Index with its 500 stocks is going to change much more often, at least once per year, and when it changes it usually does not make the financial headlines. In all of the ETFs listed above, most of the entire turnover rate is necessarily due to the change in index components.

S&P 500 vs. Dow Jones

Why should you use the Standard and Poor 500 ETF sector funds instead of Dow Jones Industry Groups ETFs? Yes, both of them use the same market to slice and dice it a slightly different way. Both the S&P and Dow Jones are very good at what they do. S&P SPDRs got into the game first in 1998 and that's when I started tracking their ETFs. Dow Jones didn't start until 2000. The SPDR funds also have a slightly lower expense ratio. Unless you have some extra time on your hands, it's not worth your time to track both sets of ETFs, because over the long term there would be very little difference in overall performance and one of the main goals of this book is to simplify your investing process.

Foreign Markets

I for one am against the conventional wisdom of investing in the Chinese market through either the mutual funds or ETFs that primarily invest in those markets. You have most likely heard how the Far East markets outperform our markets in the United States, and that it is no doubt true during selected periods of time. But they fall further and harder when they do fall. Let's just say I do not trust the Chinese at all for the following reasons:

You are bound to have heard about how they have stolen our intellectual property and time after time very little if anything is ever done about it. Some major manufacturing industries are beginning to return to the United States for primarily that very reason. Also, Chinese micro-caps have been found to have very **unreliable** financials in recent years. Yes, we can beat the U.S. based stock index averages without the volatility and uncertainty of foreign markets. When something is going wrong in our markets it will be reported sooner and we will be able to react to it quicker. With mutual funds or ETFs that invest primarily in foreign markets you will have higher fees and less reliable dividends because of currency exchange rates and many of these funds only pay dividends once or twice per year at most. So, when the dividends are cut you will have to wait longer to find out and suffer a more severe cut as a result. In addition, Asian countries, especially China manipulate their currency to keep it artificially low to help **their** exports. This in turn, means your dividends will be lower than they should be when they are converted to U.S. dollars. We can beat the Dow Jones Industrial Average and the S&P 500 Index and still keep our investment dollars primarily in the USA. There are several ways to do this without subscribing to that $300 per year newsletter or investing in China.

Performance Calculations

Again, we will use major index ETFs for comparisons instead of the indexes because the ETFs represent a real money investment that you can invest in. The way performance is calculated is by starting off with $1,000 at the beginning of year one, then add the percentage gain or loss '*at the end*' of each calendar year including dividends, (with the dividends reinvested once at the end of each year) which will give us our total return. Then we will see what we would have at the end of three years, or five years etc. on the original $1,000 investment. In other words, to see what your original $1,000 would be worth at a given time in the future if left in the ETFs or stocks used in the examples.

Beating the Indexes

There have been at least two successful ways of beating the S&P 500 index using ETFs during the last fourteen years. Let's take at look at the performance of some major ETFs based on the calendar years ending December 31. Please take a look at Spreadsheet 4.2 again. Ticker symbol (SPY) is the SPDR S&P 500 exchange traded fund. The second column group is taking each of the nine individual SPDR exchange traded funds that collectively make up the S&P 500 listed in Chapter Four, (The SPDR Nine). These nine ETFs are each purchased in *equal dollar* amounts. The third column group is the Dow Jones Industrial Average ETF (DIA). The last column group is the Rydex Equal Weight S&P 500 Index ETF, ticker symbol (RSP).

These examples are for comparative purposes only, but these ETFs could easily be purchased if desired. The Rydex Equal Weight S&P 500 ETF (RSP) was not created until 2003 so we can only compare it in a nine calendar year time frame, whereas the other ETFs are fourteen year comparisons. The longer time frame we have information on the more predictable the future is.

As you can see in Spreadsheet 4.2, the Equal Weight SPDR Nine beat the SPY in twelve out of fourteen years although 2003 and 2006 were statistical ties. To put another way the SPY only outperformed the Equal Weight SPDR Nine in two of the last fourteen years. (1999 & 2012)

One way to make this method work for you would be to purchase at least three of the 'SPDR Nine' ETFs each year until you have all nine. If you use this method you should at first purchase one ETF from each phase of the business cycle unless you have very strong convictions as to which part of the business cycle we are in. Then continue until you have all nine ETFs.

Once you have all 'SPDR Nine' ETFs, you should let the dividends accumulate until the end of the year, and then add them to your new contributions for the additional purchases. As a general rule, you should add money to the ETFs that have underperformed the previous year. This way you can keep your investment amount relatively equal in each sector. You have to take a good look at the business cycle. Look at where we have been and where we are likely headed. Buy what is *on sale*. Don't buy what has just had a long and sustained run up. Chances are the party is almost over. Learn from your mistakes and be ready the next time the opportunity presents itself. There are pundits who will give examples where the above example was all wrong, and there is no rule in investing works every time. If there were we would all be billionaires.

An old Wall Street cliché: *"The best time to buy is when there's blood in the streets"*. Please take a good look at Spreadsheets 4.3 through 4.12 again. These spreadsheets contain the performance of each of the 'SPDR Nine' over the past fourteen calendar years. As you can see there is a wide variation of performance of different sectors of the economy.

It's most likely the near future will not reflect the recent past. If and when things do change, you want to be able to recognize it and take appropriate action. As you can see when you really look at it, only two of the SPDR Nine underperformed the S&P 500 (Financial & Technology) but they did so by rather large margins. Financials had a negative return over the fourteen year period and Technology was virtually flat. They also represent the two largest sectors of the S&P 500, both at the beginning of the period and still do now but not by as large a margin. If you believe you know what phase of the business cycle we are in, you can invest accordingly with the SPDR Nine ETFs. When you do this you should buy five or six of the 'SPDR Nine' to spread the risk. If you can just avoid the market losing ETFs, you will still outperform the overall market.

Gold

No book on investing would be complete without a few words on gold ETFs. First, we must keep in mind that gold had a good run up in the inflationary 1970s. Then from 1980 until 2002 gold was in a long bear market. Today the U.S. Dollar is slowly but surely losing its status as the world's reserve currency. Many now are of the opinion the world's new reserve currency is gold. As long as most all of the major world currencies are being inflated by increasing the money supply, owning gold is a must for any investment portfolio in this current era. It's recommended that five to ten percent of your portfolio should be in a gold ETF. Gold mining stocks are not recommended, because they have not performed as well as gold ETFs even when gold prices are rising. One reason for this is that gold is sometimes hedged years in advance. What this means is even though the price is rising the gold mining companies must sell at a lower than market price. The easiest way to own gold is through three major gold ETFs. They are:

ETF Symbol	$ In Fund	Expense Ratio	Where Gold is Stored
GLD	71.05 Billion	0.40%	HBSC Bank, London
IAU	11.79 Billion	0.25%	New York, London, Toronto
SGOL	1.92 Billion	0.39%	UBS Zurich, Switzerland

Style Investing

Style investing is one ***top down*** way of taking the whole market and divide it into nine segments as follows:

Large Cap Growth	Mid Cap Growth	Small Cap Growth
Large Cap Core	Mid Cap Core	Small Cap Core
Large Cap Value	Mid Cap Value	Small Cap Value

Some investors have long used the growth vs. value concept to slice and dice the market in a different way from the ***sector investing concept*** that we have been discussing. It's done by trying to predict which group will perform better in the near term. What is bad about style investing is one, the line between growth and value can be blurred. A stock can easily go from growth to value and back again based on valuation criteria. In sector investing it would be almost unheard of for a stock to move from one sector to another. So, if you just buy and hold a style ETF the stocks in it could radically change over a three to five year period with you hardly noticing. That is not likely with sector investing. If you are going to invest mainly in ETFs, it's strongly recommend you stick with sector investing.

Spread 5.1 Yr End 31-Dec	S&P 500 SPDR Begin Price	Div Amt Per	Div Pct	SPY End Price	Gain Loss %	$Value Cumul	Yearly Ave Return 2.78%		
1998		Website				1,000	1,000		
1999	123.31	1.41	1.15%	146.88	20.26%	1,203	1,028		
2000	146.88	1.45	0.99%	131.19	-9.69%	1,086	1,056		
2001	131.19	1.03	0.79%	114.30	-12.09%	955	1,086		
2002	114.30	1.50	1.31%	88.23	-21.50%	750	1,116		
2003	88.23	1.63	1.85%	111.28	27.97%	959	1,147		
2004	111.28	2.20	1.97%	120.87	10.59%	1,061	1,178		
2005	120.87	2.15	1.78%	124.51	4.79%	1,112	1,211		
2006	124.51	2.15	1.73%	141.62	15.47%	1,284	1,245	As of 31-Dec-12	
2007	141.62	2.70	1.91%	146.21	5.15%	1,350	1,279	Cumulative Tot	
2008	146.21	2.72	1.86%	90.24	-36.42%	858	1,315	35.62%	3 yrs
2009	90.24	2.31	2.56%	111.44	26.05%	1,082	1,351	8.69%	5 yrs
2010	111.44	2.23	2.00%	125.75	14.84%	1,242	1,389	52.93%	9 yrs
2011	125.75	2.58	2.05%	125.50	1.85%	1,265	1,427	95.71%	10 yrs
2012	125.50	3.10	2.47%	142.41	15.95%	1,467	1,467	46.69%	14 yrs

Spread 5.2 Yr End 31-Dec	Dow Diamonds Begin Price	Div Amt Per	Div Pct	DIA End Price	Gain Loss %	$Value Cumul	Yearly Ave Return 4.73%		
1998		Website				1,000	1,000		
1999	91.53	1.73	1.89%	115.19	27.74%	1,277	1,047		
2000	115.19	1.57	1.36%	106.78	-5.94%	1,202	1,097		
2001	106.78	1.56	1.46%	99.80	-5.08%	1,141	1,149		
2002	99.80	2.54	2.55%	83.51	-13.78%	983	1,203		
2003	83.51	1.93	2.31%	104.57	27.53%	1,254	1,260		
2004	104.57	2.20	2.10%	107.51	4.92%	1,316	1,319		
2005	107.51	2.24	2.08%	106.95	1.56%	1,336	1,382		
2006	106.95	2.53	2.37%	124.41	18.69%	1,586	1,447	As of 31-Dec-12	
2007	124.41	2.75	2.21%	132.55	8.75%	1,725	1,516	Cumulative Tot	
2008	132.55	2.17	1.64%	87.52	-32.33%	1,167	1,587	34.01%	3 yrs
2009	87.52	2.25	2.57%	104.57	22.05%	1,425	1,662	10.68%	5 yrs
2010	104.57	2.51	2.40%	115.63	12.98%	1,610	1,741	52.23%	9 yrs
2011	115.63	2.97	2.57%	121.85	7.95%	1,737	1,823	94.13%	10 yrs
2012	121.85	3.31	2.72%	130.58	9.88%	1,909	1,909	90.91%	14 yrs

Spread 5.3 Yr End 31-Dec	S & P 500 Begin Price	Div Amt Per	Rydex Equal Weight Div Pct	End Price	Gain Loss %	R S P $Value Cumul	Yearly Ave Return 6.63%		
2003		Website				1,000	1,000		
2004	135.45	1.47	1.09%	156.16	16.38%	1,164	1,066		
2005	156.16	1.74	1.12%	165.93	7.37%	1,250	1,137		
2006	41.48	0.52	1.26%	47.34	15.38%	1,442	1,212		
2007	47.34	0.61	1.29%	47.18	0.95%	1,456	1,293		
2008	47.18	0.65	1.37%	27.80	-39.71%	878	1,378	As of 31-Dec-12	
2009	27.80	0.52	1.89%	39.53	44.08%	1,264	1,470	Cumul Tot	
2010	39.53	0.60	1.51%	47.31	21.19%	1,532	1,567	40.97%	3 yrs
2011	47.31	0.72	1.51%	46.28	-0.66%	1,522	1,671	22.46%	5 yrs
2012	46.28	0.87	1.89%	53.32	17.10%	1,782	1,782	78.25%	9 yrs

THE Ups AND Downs
of retirement investing

CHAPTER SIX
BEAT THE MARKET WITH DIVIDEND PAYING COMMON STOCKS

Since you have taken the time to read this far, you are bound to also have watched the cable TV financial channels and have seen lots of interviews with many of the financial 'experts'. Of course what usually happens is, if they get it right they are invited back. But when they get it wrong, you usually don't see them again, or if you do see them again they are not held accountable for their mistakes. There is Fox News that spends almost as much time in political bashing, if not more, than it does in reporting in real news you can use. Also, there is CNBC that has Jim Cramer that says buy this stock, sell that stock and maybe hold another. As for diversification, as long as you are in at least five different S&P sectors you are pretty well diversified. Yes, he is very entertaining and I still watch 'Mad Money'. What I have not been able to learn from watching cable TV, is how to build a lasting portfolio of common stocks, preferred stocks, Master Limited Partnerships (MLPs), ETFs and corporate bonds without signing up with one of their wealth management services.

Now we must work a little harder. You know we have to be willing to work a little harder if we want a greater reward. I know from experience that the hardest lesson to learn when investing in stocks, is knowing when to sell. Therefore, what is recommended is for you to buy good stocks that not only are industry leaders, but pay good dividends and raise their dividends year after year at a sustainable rate, and that sell decision will not have to be made nearly as often. What you shouldn't do is look for the highest yielders that have unsustainable dividends. Examples of these would be Pitney Bowes (PB), a postage machine maker and some rural telephone companies that are losing customers to the larger telecoms that offer cell phone and computer services.

It's also strongly recommended that you stick with U.S. based dividend paying common stocks, especially in tax advantaged accounts. According to a recent article in Barron's there are now over 400 companies in the S&P 500 that pays a dividend. This is the highest number since 1999.

I know from personal experience that countries like Japan, New Zealand and France have taxed the dividends paid to me in the past, up to 15% in my tax advantaged accounts. I don't know of any way for you to get any kind of tax credit in your tax advantaged accounts for this under current IRS regulations, or tax treaties with these foreign governments. Another bit of bad news came to light recently, is that transfer agents and banks that sponsor American Depositary Receipts (ADRs) can now charge you a yearly custody fee, which is withheld from your dividend if one is paid. If a dividend is not paid, this fee will be taken from your cash account anyway. An ADR is a foreign stock that has been grouped from the foreign stock shares and sold on U.S. exchanges. There could be two or three shares of this foreign stock to one ADR share and sold on U.S. exchanges, quoted in U.S. dollars. Besides these extra fees there is the currency risk that always comes with owning foreign based stocks. I currently do not own any ADRs nor do I recommend them.

Currently you can buy British based common stocks and there will not be any tax withheld on the dividends paid in tax advantaged accounts. Be sure and check to see what the current tax withholding agreements are with a foreign based company stock that you are considering. The only thing certain about our tax laws and tax treaties with other countries is that they are constantly changing. However, in your taxable account, a U.S. investor can normally use the foreign dividend withholding taxes for a credit towards his or her own U.S. tax liabilities. Please verify with your tax advisor.

Trading Stocks and ETFs

You need to understand how the system works when putting in the buy or sell order for any issue. First there is the ***Bid / Asked Spread*** also known as just the ***Spread***. The spread is what the market makers make when a stock or ETF, etc. is traded. It's the difference in price when the market makers bring a buyer and a seller together. For example: If I were to sell 100 shares of General Electric at $22.25 per share, and you were to buy my shares, you would have to pay a little more, maybe only $22.26 on a heavily traded stock such as GE. We will still both be charged a commission on this buy/sell transaction. In small cap or thinly traded stocks the spread can be much more. TD Ameritrade shows you both the bid and the asked current prices, when you are considering a trade. Most of the other on line discount brokers does also.

Limit Orders

When buying stocks with your on line broker you want to be sure to use *limit orders*. A limit order is: when you sell, it is the minimum amount you will accept. When you buy a stock it is the most you are willing to pay. If you were to put in a *market order*, you might be charged much more than the quoted price on a buy order, or sell at much less on your sell order. Both of my discount brokers allow customers to use limit orders without an additional charge above market orders for on line trades.

All-or-None-Order

Another thing to keep in mind when placing an order, either buy or sell, especially late in the trading day, is to use an "All-or-None Order". An all-or-none order is just that. Either a specified quantity of your shares at a specified price (or better) will be bought or sold or none of them will. For example, if you don't use the all-or-none you could put in an order to buy 200 shares of a $50.00 issue and only get an execution of 5 shares and still be charged a full commission. An all-or-none order is good for the entire trading day, unless cancelled by you first.

Fill-or-Kill-Order

This is an order to buy or sell a specified quantity of your shares at a specified price (or better) immediately. If the order can't be done immediately the order will be cancelled.

Value Investing

I'm more of a value investor than a growth investor and this is why: study after study has shown that over the long term value investing beats growth investing in both large cap and small cap stocks. In addition, long term studies have shown that lower P/E stocks (value) have outperformed higher P/E stocks. I know there are periods of time when growth beats value, by a large margin such as in the 1999-2000 tech bubble, but when the party is over it will be like falling off a cliff. That being said, some of the stocks I follow and own could be classified as growth. I don't know and I don't even bother to check because, for one reason, before you read this, the stock could go from value to growth or vice versa. What should matter most to you is the stocks you want to own are leaders in their industry and they raise their dividend on a regular basis at a rate higher than the inflation rate.

One of the greatest investor in the last fifty years, Warren Buffet, would not invest in technology companies during the go-go 1990s. He's still one of the greatest investors in at least fifty years. Also, it should be acknowledged that small cap stocks have outperformed large caps over the long term. But, the downside to that is small cap stocks have been more volatile and on average they pay a much smaller dividend if they pay one at all, many pay less than 1%.

Initial Public Offerings (IPOs)

I have never bought an IPO and I doubt if I ever will. Do you remember the recent Facebook (FB) offering? It traded at over $38.00 per share under all the hype the first day of trading. This is usually what happens especially with a new glamour company. If you had just waited a couple of months you could have bought that same share of stock for under $18.00 per share. Another recent example is Groupon Inc. (GRPN). Soon after its IPO in November 2011 Groupon's common stock was selling at $31.14 per share. Just one year later in November 2012 the stock was trading at $2.60 per share. That is more than a 91% loss in value.

Another example is Boston Chicken which later changed its name to Boston Market after it went public in 1993 with a 143% gain in its first few days of trading. It was trading at $50.00 per share. Later on, in 1998 it was trading at $0.50 per share before filing bankruptcy. That's a loss of 99%. The fact that you love the product or service of a new company is not necessarily a reason to buy the common stock. Let's keep in mind that the private equity people and the underwriters have determined that the value has peaked—at least in the short term. That's why the stock is brought public in the first place. It's a big payday for the underwriters and private equity. There have been a few IPO successes, but all you really have to go on is a lot of hype. It reminds me of political promises, buyer beware.

S & P 1500 Dividend Aristocrats

You are very likely to have heard of the S & P Dividend Aristocrats. These are publicly traded stocks that have raised their dividends in *each* of the last 25 years. If they fail to increase their dividend in one of those years they are out of the Index. There is even an ETF that tracks this index (SDY). One of the good things about this ETF is that it pays a higher dividend than any of the S&P 500 Index funds. Another good thing is that it is well diversified over most of the S&P sectors. One thing I don't like about it is that there are some stocks in it that should not be invested in individually. But this is also true with just about any stock ETF.

According to Ned Davis Research, over the last forty years ending December 31, 2011, dividend paying stocks have outperformed growth stocks by a margin of at least six to one. The outperformance is by over 7% per year according to this major study. (8.61% to 1.35%). When we are in a bear market (downturn) the margin is even greater, by over 12% on an annual basis. When you invest in dividend payers that increase the dividends on average at least once per year, the outperformance is greater still. By following this system you will win by not losing. I know the pundits will ask how you will find the next Apple, Microsoft, Home Depot or Wal-Mart in their early stages. The answer is you probably won't, but neither will you do the hundreds of trades it will take you to do so (and then only if you are extremely lucky). In other words, about the same odds as hitting the multi-million dollar lottery.

In 2012 the S&P Value ETF (IVE) outperformed the S&P Growth ETF (IVW) . The S&P Growth ETF (IVW) has outperformed the S&P Value ETF (IVE) during each of the five previous calendar years (2007 through 2011). In the six calendar years (2001 through 2006) prior to this the value ETF (IVE) outperformed the growth ETF (IVW). When making comparisons like this here is another cliché to keep in mind. *"In the long run it all reverts to the mean"*. In other words a period of outperformance will likely be followed by a period of underperformance. Even during this period of growth stock index outperformance, my portfolio of selected dividend paying (mostly value) stocks have outperformed the S&P 500 Large Cap Growth Index ETF (IVW).

Dividend Reinvestment Plans (DRIPS)

When it comes to Dividend Reinvestment Plans commonly known as DRIPs, I don't like them any better than I like drips in my household plumbing. Why? One reason is it's a record keeping nightmare. For example, if you buy 100 shares of SPY you will remember that better than 102 shares after one year and 103 shares after year two, etc. Reason two, is that all of your holdings will not be *'on sale'* at the time of your purchase just because it's the end of the quarter or the end of the year. You should not want to buy even one or two shares after a hopefully big run up in price. It's better for you to give more thought to your buy decisions and to keep you engaged in the investing process. It's better to let your cash pile up a little and add the cash to your contributions and buy what is *on sale*. A third reason, is the commission will in all probability be higher on the additional very few shares you would be purchasing whenever the dividends are paid.

You should keep a record of all your portfolios on a spreadsheet just to keep your brokerage firm honest, and give yourself peace of mind. I haven't had any disputes with any of my brokers the last twenty years, but prior to that my 401k brokerage misplaced $10,000 after selling a stock and it took me six months to get it corrected. So, it can happen.

General Electric—Averaging Down

Investing can be much like playing sports. Sometimes you get knocked down. Then you must decide whether to get back up and fight on or just quit. In 2008 it was just such a year, and many of us investors faced a lot of tough investment decisions with the market in a freefall. In April 2008 I bought 140 shares of General Electric (GE) at $32.42 per share. Then in June 2008 it fell down to $30.23 and I bought another 210 shares. With the annual dividend at $1.24 a share, this gave me an average dividend of about 4%. On March 2, 2009 after the dividend had been cut from $0.31 per quarter to just $0.10 per quarter the common stock fell to $7.06 per share. In the next week when GE started rising towards $9.00 per share, I decided to take the plunge and I bought another 750 shares at $8.73 per share. These new shares, even after the dividend cut, were paying me a 4.58% dividend. The first purchases were only paying me 3.82% dividend when I bought them. By doing this I averaged my shares down to $15.88 per share for the entire 1,100 shares. As we go to press I still own 650 shares and the stock is selling at over $22.00 per share.

GE is a very large company with many divisions. Its common stock was taken down mostly by its financial unit. Other divisions of GE were doing relatively well. By averaging down, I was able to turn a losing stock into a winner much quicker. I've made up all my losses and then some, even though the stock price has not completely recovered.

If you have at least $50,000 in your brokerage accounts, it is highly recommend that you buy dividend paying stocks. These stocks should come from at least seven different sectors of 'The SPDR Nine'. Let's take a look at some of the leading stocks derived from the SPDR Nine ETF, most of which I currently own in my personal portfolios. You should compare the sector and major index averages to these leaders.

Consumer Discretionary XLY
McDonalds (MCD)
V F Corp (VFC)

Consumer Staples XLP
Proctor & Gamble (PG)
General Mills (GIS)
Altria (MO)

Energy XLE
Chevron (CVX)
ConocoPhillips (COP)
Royal Dutch Shell (RDS-B)*

Financial XLF
Health Care REIT (HCN)
Realty Income (O)
Wells Fargo (WFC)
BB&T Bank (BBT)

Industrial XLI
General Electric (GE)
United Parcel Service (UPS)
Emerson Electric (EMR)

---

* Shell Oil is a foreign company but its 'B' shares pay quarterly dividends in U.S. dollars, not from a converted currency and no foreign tax is withheld.

Materials XLB
Air Products & Chemicals (APD)
RPM International (RPM) S&P Midcap 400
DuPont (DD)

Technology XLK
Intel (INTC)
Verizon (VZ)
AT&T (T)

Health Care XLV
Abbot Labs (ABT)
Johnson & Johnson (JNJ)

Utilities XLU
American Electric Power (AEP)
Southern Co (SO)
Westar Energy (WR) S&P Midcap 400
ONEOK (OKE)

Now you are probably wondering, how I came upon these stocks and how can I justify them being leaders. One way is by looking at the charts (technical analysis). It's good for making comparisons when the issues you are comparing pay close to the same dividend percentage. Most of these stocks have both outperformed their comparable ETF, and the S&P 500, and pay a higher comparable dividend. When the two or more stocks or ETFs you are comparing pay vastly different dividend percentages we have to find a different way to compare performance, because most charts only compare the index averages or stock prices. They do not take dividends into consideration unless it is a ***total returns*** chart.

There are other spreadsheets at the end of this chapter that takes care of this problem. This is a little (maybe a lot depending upon your perspective) more work. But by doing this homework you will learn a lot and have a leg up on those who don't know how or don't take the time to do this research. Now, let's look at how this spreadsheet (6.1) works in detail so you will understand completely. We will use McDonalds as the example on Spreadsheet 6.1.

Column (A) is the calendar year ending December 31. (Vertical)

Column (C) line two is the SPDR ETF that the stock is derived from. (Horizontal)

Column (B) is the market trading symbol of the stock. (MCD)

Column (C) is the closing stock price of the last trading day of the prior year. This amount could be different from the previous year close due to a stock split.

Column (D) is the dividend amount you would have received if you had owned this stock the entire calendar year.

Now please look at:

Column (I) Row four, this is the average total return per year you would have received if you had owned the stock the entire time period (usually fourteen years).

Column (E) is the dividend percentage you would have received based on the stock price at the beginning of the year.

Column (F) is the closing stock price at the end of the last trading day of the year.

Column (G) is the percentage gain or loss you would have received by owning the stock the entire year including the dividend (total return).

Column (H) is the nominal dollar value the stock would be worth if you just bought and held the stock and reinvested the dividends once per year at the end of each year.

Column (I) is the average annual return you have received had you owned the stock the entire period (usually fourteen years), by just buying and holding and reinvesting the dividends once per year at the end of each year. Note: the rows of the current year in columns (H) and (I) should be equal dollar amount (3,033) in the McDonalds example. This column is a check figure to calculate the average annual total return.

Column (J) is the earnings per share reported (EPS) for the fiscal year ending during or at the end of the calendar year. A word of caution about the EPS, most large corporations are restating their earnings for both current year and two to three years in the past on a regular basis. So when you check current year earnings don't be surprised to find that the past few years earnings amounts do not agree with what is recorded.

Column (K) is price per share divided by the earnings per share (P/E Ratio). This column is adjusted for stock splits where applicable.

Now please take a look below the solid black line for the cumulative totals. We use the exchange traded funds for the Dow Jones Industrial

Average (DIA). For the S&P 500 we use SPY and then we use XLY for the Consumers Discretionary SPDR exchange traded fund. I use five, ten, and fourteen year periods for comparisons.

As you can see with the five year comparison, the DIA had a cumulative total return of 10.68%, SPY had a comparative return of 8.69%, and the Consumer Discretionary ETF (XLY) had a comparative return of 56.89%. McDonald's cumulative total return of 72.94% for the five year period compares favorably with The DIA and SPY as well as with the exchange traded fund that McDonald's is a component of (XLY). Next look at the ten and fourteen year lines below and follow the same format. When you look on the next two lines and compare the ten and fourteen year periods McDonalds compares quite favorably to all three of the *market* ETFs.

The basic philosophy is to look for stocks in each sector of 'The SPDR Nine' that pay above average dividends (at least 2.8%). They should also increase their dividends at a rate above the inflation rate and have outperformed the major indexes, and hold them for the long term. In the next few pages of this chapter there is a little commentary on most of the stocks that I track from each sector of the 'SPDR Nine'. In addition, there is the ETF sector that each stock is derived from and my commentary on why each of these stocks merits our close attention. In all cases this is a long term outlook. At the end of this chapter are the spreadsheets that show the performance of each stock from the last fourteen years.

McDonalds: XLY Consumer Discretionary

It's the number one fast food company in the world in sales. Many restaurants come and go but McDonalds has stood the test of time and just look at that great financial performance.

See Spreadsheet 6.1.

VF Corporation: XLY Consumer Discretionary

VFC has all kinds of apparel from all over the world, just look in your closet and most likely you have some of their brands like North Face, Timberland, Wrangler and Lee. With the recent run up in price the dividend is now below 2% as we go to press. You should wait for a pullback before you consider buying this stock. See Spreadsheet 6.2.

Proctor & Gamble: XLP Consumer Staples

Proctor & Gamble has been in business since 1837 and has been paying a dividend since 1890. Not many (if any) companies can match this record. The good news is PG has had only two negative return years in the last twenty years. The not so good news is the returns have been low the last few years. In my opinion, one reason for the recent underperformance is the integration of Gillette into their vast product line. Its current dividend of over 3% is in an historical high range for them. I currently own the stock and I don't have any current plans to sell it. See Spreadsheet 6.3.

Altria (Phillip Morris): XLP Consumer Staples

Altria is now just a domestic tobacco company. It split off its old Kraft Foods and International Tobacco units as well as Miller Brewing. It still has had great financial performance in recent years as well as in the long term past. It currently pays a dividend in excess of 5%. The question is how long this can continue with domestic tobacco use in decline and the anti-smoking health concerns we all have. I sold my shares in early 2012 because I needed to raise some cash. As of today (Early 2013) I'm neutral on this stock See Spreadsheet 6.4.

General Mills: XLP Consumer Staples

General Mills started with two flower mills in 1860. Since then their products such as Cheerios, Wheaties, Green Giant, Pillsbury, Nature Valley and many others have became household names. Back in 2002 GIS had a negative total return of -7.61% and that was the worst performance in the last twenty years. As you can see on the spreadsheet they have outperformed the Dow, S&P 500, and Consumer Staples sector fund for the five, ten, and fourteen year tracking periods. This is a 'Steady Eddie' stock that currently yields over 3% and that I will continue to keep in my portfolio. See Spreadsheet 6.5.

Chevron: XLE Energy

Chevron is a major integrated oil and gas company, with both production and refining operations. It has a great financial performance record and currently pays a dividend of over 3% and it has been raising the dividend at least once and sometimes twice per year in recent years.

It has outperformed its major indexes over the past five, ten, and fourteen year periods. It's one of my core holdings. See Spreadsheet 6.6.

ConocoPhillips: XLE Energy

ConocoPhillips is a major integrated oil and gas company. It recently spun off its refining operations. Its financial performance record has not been as good as Chevron or Shell, but at least they did not reduce the dividend after the spinoff. On the other hand, it has not done very well in the recent past (five years) but it has done better than the overall market over the past, ten and fourteen year periods. I own this oil company too along with Chevron and Shell 'B'. ConocoPhillips would probably be the first oil stock that I would sell. See Spreadsheet 6.7.

Royal Dutch Shell 'B': XLE Energy

Shell ('B' shares) is the other major oil company that I believe you should consider owning. It's a foreign company (Dutch) that pays the dividend in U.S. dollars (The 'B' shares). So there is no dividend currency risk to worry about. These 'B' shares have only been trading on the NYSE since 2005. They have outperformed both the Dow 30 and the S&P 500 and it has outperformed its peer group ETF (XLE) by a smaller amount during this period. See Spreadsheet 6.8.

Realty Income: XLF Financial

This company owns about 2,700 commercial properties in forty-eight states. Realty Income is known as the monthly dividend company. Its corporate structure is a REIT. Real Estate Investment Trusts are required to pay out 90% of their profits in dividends each year. It has been paying a monthly dividend for over forty-three years. One small caveat is the record keeping of a monthly dividend that is currently 0.1809167 per month. Yes, that is seven decimal places. This dividend is usually raised every quarter. Its share price held up very well in the real estate meltdown of 2008. This is a very well managed company that has only had two negative calendar years of less than -10.00% each, in the last eighteen years. It currently pays a 4.9% dividend as we go to press. I own this stock. See Spreadsheet 6.9.

Health Care REIT: XLF Financial

As its name indicates this company invests in senior living facilities, medical office buildings, as well as inpatient and outpatient medical care facilities. It was founded in 1970. This company has had only one slightly down year (-4.69% in 2005) since 1999. It even had a positive return throughout the financial meltdown. It currently pays about a 4.7% dividend. Since 1992 it has raised its dividend every year except 2007 when they had a slight decrease. I also own this REIT. See Spreadsheet 6.10.

Wells Fargo: XLF Financial

Wells Fargo is one of the better managed money center banks. It has over 9,000 locations in thirty-nine states. This bank actually outperformed the overall market during the financial crisis. It has also outperformed its peer group as well as the in the last five years. I currently own this stock. See Spreadsheet 6.11.

BB&T Bank: XLF Financial

BB&T is a smaller regional bank that has over 1,700 locations in the southeast and mid-Atlantic states. This bank stock has only been an average performer in the short term and an underperformer to the overall market in the ten and fourteen year periods. I sold my shares in the summer of 2012. See Spreadsheet 6.12.

Citigroup: XLF Financial

This is one stock that growth and momentum investors will hold up to us and say buy and hold investing just doesn't work. This is certainly a good/bad example, it's just an exception and there are no absolutes that will work every time. Yes, it's time for your author to fess up. I used to own this stock and yes I lost much more on it than I would like to admit. This example is put in to show that nothing will work for you every time and I'm certainly not perfect. Citibank is a 200 year old money center bank with branches all over the world. They took billions of dollars in bailout money from our federal government. Prior to the financial crisis it had been a great long term performer that paid a 4% dividend. See Spreadsheet 6.13.

General Electric: XLI Industrial

GE is a conglomerate that could easily fit into two different sectors of the S&P 500. It is listed in the Industrial sector. GE has been in business since 1892. Its manufacturing would of course be in the Industrial sector and GE Capital would be in the financial sector. GE's long term performance has been better than the financial sector but not as good as the Industrial sector. See Spreadsheet 6.14.

United Parcel Service: XLI Industrial

If you are looking for a second or third industrial stock to round out your portfolio, UPS is definitely a leader in the package delivery business. It has been just a little better than a market performer during the last five years, but not as well with the ten year period comparison.

See Spreadsheet 6.15.

Emerson Electric: XLI Industrial

Emerson Electric got its start making fans and electric motors. Today it is a global leader in automating industrial processes and technological fields. Emerson Electric has showed it is very shareholder friendly, by raising its dividend every year for fifty-five straight years. This is the type of stock I like to buy and hold forever. They have managed to raise the dividend even when earnings fell. Even though it has been a bit cyclical by falling 33% in 2008 it turned out to be a buying opportunity. See Spreadsheet 6.16.

RPM International: XLB Materials

RPM is a midcap stock in the S&P 400 Midcap Index. It's a specialty chemical company that sells its products all over the world. RPM has raised its dividend each and every year for more than twenty years. It has outperformed its sector ETF as well as the Dow and the S&P 500 over this period. It's currently paying a 2.9% dividend. I currently own RPM common stock in my IRA. See Spreadsheet 6.17.

Air Products and Chemicals: XLB Materials

Air Products is an S&P 500 company that currently pays a dividend of almost 3%. It has been close to a market performer and might be a good stock for diversification. See Spreadsheet 6.18.

DuPont: XLB Materials

The good news about DuPont is that its dividend was finally raised for the first time since 2007. They have been profitable for each of the last ten years, but their total return has averaged less that 3% per year for the last fourteen years. DuPont currently pays an above average dividend of 3.6%. Even though I don't see much downside risk to this stock I do not plan to own it. See Spreadsheet 6.19.

Intel: XLK Technology

Intel is the leader in the estimated $30 billion computer processing industry. It is the world's largest semiconductor company. Intel has a sector leading dividend of over 4% Intel got serious about paying dividends in 2007 when they first exceeded 2%. Since then they have steadily increased the dividend to over 4% here in 2013. Like many stocks, especially in the Technology Sector the price to earnings ratio (P/E) has come down from a (believe it or not) high of 158 in 2001 to 8.8 in 2011. With a shareholder friendly dividend policy I expect this stock to be a 'Steady Eddie' performer going forward. See Spreadsheet 6.20.

Verizon: XLK Technology-(Telecom)

Verizon is a major telecom company that provides internet, and cell phone services and was formerly known as Bell Atlantic. It has a way above average dividend in the 4.8% range. On a total return basis it has been close to an average market performer. See Spreadsheet 6.21.

AT&T: XLK Technology-(Telecom)

AT&T is the other major telecom company that is a direct competitor of Verizon. It was formerly known as SBC Communications. The best thing to say about this average performer is its current 5.3% dividend. See Spreadsheet 6.22.

Johnson & Johnson: XLV Health Care

Johnson & Johnson is a major pharmaceutical and medical supply company. It has been an average market performer over the past ten years with an above average 3.3% dividend. The dividend has been increased each year for the past twenty years. The really good thing about JNJ is that it has very little downside risk although recently, growth has been slow at best. See Spreadsheet 6.23.

Abbott Labs: XLV Health Care

Abbott Labs has been a similar performer to fellow big pharma company Johnson & Johnson. It has performed a little better in 2010-2011. As we go to press it has started trading as two companies in early 2013. Due to the uncertainty of this split, I would not buy either of these new stock issues before mid 2013 at the soonest. See Spreadsheet 6.24.

Southern Company: XLU Utilities

Southern Company is the second largest holding in S&P 500 Utilities Sector ETF. It is headquartered in Atlanta, GA. As you probably know the southeast U.S. is one of the largest population growth areas in the country. It has been a better than average over the last fourteen years with an average total return of over 11% per year. As you can see on the spreadsheet the worst year it had was a negative 10% back in 1999. See Spreadsheet 6.25.

ONEOK: XLU Utilities

ONEOK is the holding company for three natural gas utility companies in Kansas, Texas and Oklahoma. It also is the general partner in ONEOK Partners L.P. and owns 43% of the partnership units. I bought this stock in February 2005 and sold it in November 2011. My total return was almost 30% per year. In 2012 ONEOK only gained 1.5% in total return. What scared me was the P/E ratio recently jumped from 12 to 26. The stock has continued to grow but at a slower rate. I'll wait for a pullback before considering a repurchase. See Spreadsheet 6.26.

American Electric Power: XLU Utilities

American Electric Power has been in business since 1906 and its headquarters is in Columbus, Ohio. It has operations in Ohio, Virginia, West Virginia, Indiana, Kentucky, Tennessee, Arkansas, Oklahoma, and Michigan. I currently own this stock mainly because when I bought it, it had a P/E of 10 while the Utility Sector average P/E was about 16. As we go to press both P/Es are about 14. Its current dividend is over 4%. See Spreadsheet 6.27.

Westar Energy: XLU Utilities

Westar Energy is the largest electric utility in Kansas. Two former executives were charged with looting the company in the early 2000s. One trial ended in a hung jury while the second trial ended with the conviction overturned. Needless to say, the stock suffered for several years. The dividend was cut by 37% in 2003. With new management I believe the company is now on the right track. It has performed well in the last 7-8 years. Its current dividend is about 4.5%. I currently own this stock. See Spreadsheet 6.28.

	A	B	C	D	E	F	G	H	I	J	K
1		Spreadsheet 6.1 McDonalds				Split Adjusted			Yearly		
2	Year		X L Y	S&P Consumer Discreationary ETF					Ave	Year End	
3	Ending		Begin		Div	End	Gain		Tot Ret	E P S	P / E
4	31-Dec	Sym	Price	Div	Pct	Price	Loss	$ Value	8.25%		
5	1998					38.41		1,000	1,000		
6	1999	MCD	38.41	0.20	0.51%	40.31	5.45%	1,055	1,082		
7	2000	MCD	40.31	0.22	0.53%	34.00	-15.12%	895	1,172	1.46	27.61
8	2001	MCD	34.00	0.23	0.66%	26.47	-21.49%	703	1,268	1.25	27.20
9	2002	MCD	26.47	0.24	0.89%	16.08	-38.36%	433	1,373	0.77	34.38
10	2003	MCD	16.08	0.40	2.49%	24.83	56.90%	680	1,486	1.18	13.63
11	2004	MCD	24.83	0.55	2.22%	32.06	31.33%	893	1,609	1.79	13.87
12	2005	MCD	32.06	0.67	2.09%	33.72	7.27%	957	1,741	2.02	15.87
13	2006	MCD	33.72	1.00	2.97%	44.33	34.43%	1,287	1,885	2.29	14.72
14	2007	MCD	44.33	1.50	3.38%	58.91	36.27%	1,754	2,041	1.93	22.97
15	2008	MCD	58.91	1.63	2.76%	62.19	8.33%	1,900	2,209	3.76	15.67
16	2009	MCD	62.19	2.05	3.30%	62.44	3.70%	1,970	2,391	4.11	15.13
17	2010	MCD	62.44	2.26	3.62%	76.76	26.55%	2,494	2,588	4.58	13.63
18	2011	MCD	76.76	2.53	3.30%	100.33	34.00%	3,341	2,802	5.27	14.57
19	2012	MCD	100.33	2.87	2.86%	88.21	-9.22%	3,033	3,033		
					DIA	SPY	XLY	2012	Cumul	Fiscal yr end	
				Cumulative	10.68%	8.69%	56.89%	72.94%	5 yr	31-Dec	
				Cumulative	94.13%	95.71%	131.69%	600.27%	10 yr		
				Cumulative	90.91%	46.69%	110.98%	203.33%	14 yr		

		Spreadsheet 6.2	V F Corporation					Yearly		
Year		X L Y	S&P Consumer Discreationary ETF					Ave	Year End	
Ending		Begin		Div	End	Gain		Tot Ret	E P S	P / E
31-Dec	Sym	Price	Div	Pct	Price	Loss	$ Value	11.36%		
1998	VFC				46.88		1,000	1,000		
1999	VFC	46.88	0.85	1.81%	30.00	-34.19%	658	1,114		
2000	VFC	30.00	0.44	1.47%	36.24	22.27%	805	1,240	2.26	13.27
2001	VFC	36.24	0.47	1.30%	39.01	8.94%	877	1,381	1.89	19.17
2002	VFC	39.01	0.97	2.49%	36.05	-5.10%	832	1,538	3.24	12.04
2003	VFC	36.05	1.01	2.80%	43.24	22.75%	1,021	1,713	3.09	11.67
2004	VFC	43.24	1.05	2.43%	55.38	30.50%	1,332	1,907	3.52	12.28
2005	VFC	55.38	1.10	1.99%	55.34	1.91%	1,358	2,124	4.21	13.15
2006	VFC	55.34	1.94	3.51%	82.08	51.83%	2,062	2,365	4.73	11.70
2007	VFC	82.08	2.23	2.72%	68.66	-13.63%	1,781	2,634	5.41	15.17
2008	VFC	68.66	2.32	3.38%	54.77	-16.85%	1,481	2,933	5.42	12.67
2009	VFC	54.77	2.37	4.33%	73.24	38.05%	2,044	3,266	4.13	13.26
2010	VFC	73.24	2.43	3.32%	86.18	20.99%	2,473	3,637	5.18	14.14
2011	VFC	86.18	2.61	3.03%	126.99	50.38%	3,719	4,050	7.98	10.80
2012	VFC	126.99	3.03	2.39%	150.97	21.27%	4,510	4,510		
				DIA	SPY	XLY	2012	Cumul	Fiscal yr end	
			Cumulative	10.68%	8.69%	56.89%	153.27%	5 yr	31-Jan	
			Cumulative	94.13%	95.71%	131.69%	442.17%	10 yr		
			Cumulative	90.91%	46.69%	110.98%	350.98%	14 yr		

Spreadsheet 6.3 Proctor & Gamble

Year Ending 31-Dec	Sym	XLP Begin Price	Div	S&P Consumer Staples ETF Div Pct	End Price	Gain Loss	$ Value	Yearly Ave Tot Ret 5.12%	Year End EPS	P/E
1998	PG				91.31		1,000	1,000		
1999	PG	91.31	1.20	1.31%	109.56	21.30%	1,213	1,051		
2000	PG	109.56	1.34	1.22%	78.44	-27.18%	883	1,105	1.23	44.54
2001	PG	78.44	1.46	1.86%	79.13	2.74%	908	1,162	1.04	37.71
2002	PG	79.13	1.89	2.39%	85.94	10.99%	1,007	1,221	1.54	25.69
2003	PG	85.94	1.74	2.02%	99.88	18.25%	1,191	1,284	1.84	23.35
2004	PG	49.94	0.98	1.96%	55.08	12.25%	1,337	1,349	2.15	23.23
2005	PG	55.08	1.09	1.98%	57.88	7.06%	1,431	1,418	2.48	22.21
2006	PG	57.88	1.21	2.09%	64.27	13.13%	1,619	1,491	2.64	21.92
2007	PG	64.27	1.36	2.12%	73.42	16.35%	1,884	1,567	2.96	21.71
2008	PG	73.42	1.55	2.11%	61.82	-13.69%	1,626	1,648	3.56	20.62
2009	PG	61.82	1.72	2.78%	60.63	0.86%	1,640	1,732	3.58	17.27
2010	PG	60.63	1.89	3.11%	64.33	9.21%	1,791	1,821	3.53	17.18
2011	PG	64.33	2.06	3.20%	66.71	6.90%	1,915	1,914	3.93	16.37
2012	PG	66.71	2.21	3.31%	67.89	5.08%	2,012	2,012		
				DIA	SPY	XLP	2012	Cumul	Fiscal yr end	
			Cumulative	10.68%	8.69%	38.87%	6.79%	5 yr	30-Jun	
			Cumulative	94.13%	95.71%	119.42%	99.76%	10 yr		
			Cumulative	90.91%	46.69%	70.79%	101.22%	14 yr		

Spreadsheet 6.4 Altria (Philip Morris)

Year Ending 31-Dec	Sym	XLP Begin Price	Div	S&P Consumer Staples ETF Div Pct	End Price	Gain Loss	$ Value	Yearly Ave Tot Ret 14.39%	Year End EPS	P/E
1998	MO				53.50		1,000	1,000		
1999	MO	53.50	1.88	3.51%	23.00	-53.50%	465	1,144		
2000	MO	23.00	2.02	8.78%	44.00	100.09%	930	1,309	3.75	6.13
2001	MO	44.00	2.17	4.93%	45.85	9.14%	1,016	1,497	3.88	11.34
2002	MO	45.85	2.44	5.32%	40.53	-6.28%	952	1,712	5.18	8.85
2003	MO	40.53	2.64	6.51%	54.42	40.78%	1,340	1,959	4.48	9.05
2004	MO	54.42	2.82	5.18%	61.10	17.46%	1,574	2,241	4.57	11.91
2005	MO	61.10	3.06	5.01%	72.00	22.85%	1,933	2,563	3.91	15.63
2006	MO	72.00	3.32	4.61%	85.82	23.81%	2,394	2,932	1.51	47.68
2007	MO	85.82	24.96	29.08%	75.58	17.15%	2,804	3,354	1.30	66.02
2008	MO	75.58	52.74	69.78%	15.06	-10.29%	2,516	3,836	1.45	52.12
2009	MO	15.06	1.32	8.76%	19.63	39.11%	3,499	4,388	1.54	9.78
2010	MO	19.63	1.42	7.23%	24.62	32.65%	4,642	5,020	1.94	10.12
2011	MO	24.62	1.55	6.30%	29.65	26.73%	5,883	5,742	1.64	15.01
2012	MO	29.65	1.67	5.63%	31.44	11.67%	6,569	6,569		
Includes Asset Sales in 2007-08				DIA	SPY	XLP	2012	Cumul	Fiscal yr end	
			Cumul	10.68%	8.69%	38.87%	134.26%	5 yr	31-Dec	
			Cumul	94.13%	95.71%	119.42%	590.23%	10 yr		
			Cumul	90.91%	46.69%	70.79%	556.91%	14 yr		

Spreadsheet 6.5 General Mills

Year Ending 31-Dec	Sym	XLP Begin Price	Div	S&P Consumer Staples ETF Div Pct	End Price	Gain Loss	$ Value	Yearly Ave Tot Ret 8.34%	Year End EPS	P/E
1998	GIS				75.62		1,000	1,000		
1999	GIS	37.81	1.10	2.91%	35.75	-2.54%	975	1,083		
2000	GIS	35.75	1.10	3.08%	44.56	27.72%	1,245	1,174	2.00	17.88
2001	GIS	44.56	1.10	2.47%	52.01	19.19%	1,484	1,272	2.28	19.54
2002	GIS	52.01	1.10	2.11%	46.95	-7.61%	1,371	1,378	1.35	38.53
2003	GIS	46.95	1.10	2.34%	45.30	-1.17%	1,355	1,493	2.43	19.32
2004	GIS	45.30	1.17	2.58%	49.71	12.32%	1,521	1,617	2.60	17.42
2005	GIS	49.71	1.28	2.57%	49.32	1.79%	1,549	1,752	3.08	16.14
2006	GIS	49.32	1.38	2.80%	57.60	19.59%	1,852	1,898	2.90	17.01
2007	GIS	57.60	1.52	2.64%	57.00	1.60%	1,882	2,057	3.18	18.11
2008	GIS	57.00	1.65	2.89%	60.75	9.47%	2,060	2,228	3.71	15.36
2009	GIS	60.75	1.80	2.96%	71.98	21.45%	2,502	2,414	3.80	15.99
2010	GIS	35.99	1.05	2.92%	35.59	1.81%	2,547	2,616	2.24	16.07
2011	GIS	35.59	1.17	3.29%	40.41	16.83%	2,976	2,834	2.71	13.13
2012	GIS	40.41	1.27	3.14%	40.42	3.17%	3,070	3,070		
				DIA	SPY	XLP	2012	Cumul	Fiscal yr end	
			Cumulative	10.68%	8.69%	38.87%	63.15%	5 yr	31-May	
			Cumulative	94.13%	95.71%	119.42%	123.96%	10 yr		
			Cumulative	90.91%	46.69%	70.79%	206.98%	14 yr		

Spreadsheet 6.6 Chevron

Year Ending 31-Dec	Sym	XLE Begin Price	Div	S&P Energy ETF Div Pct	End Price	Gain Loss	$ Value	Yearly Ave Tot Ret 10.72%	Year End EPS	P/E
1998	CVX				80.01		1,000	1,000		
1999	CVX	80.01	2.48	3.10%	85.90	10.46%	1,105	1,107		
2000	CVX	85.90	2.60	3.03%	84.44	1.33%	1,119	1,226	3.61	11.90
2001	CVX	84.44	2.65	3.14%	89.61	9.26%	1,223	1,357	1.85	22.82
2002	CVX	89.61	2.80	3.12%	66.48	-22.69%	945	1,503	0.52	86.16
2003	CVX	66.48	2.86	4.30%	86.39	34.25%	1,269	1,664	3.55	9.36
2004	CVX	43.20	1.53	3.54%	52.51	25.11%	1,588	1,843	6.14	7.04
2005	CVX	52.51	1.75	3.33%	52.74	3.77%	1,648	2,040	6.55	8.02
2006	CVX	52.74	2.01	3.81%	73.53	43.23%	2,360	2,259	7.80	6.76
2007	CVX	73.53	2.26	3.07%	91.00	26.83%	2,994	2,501	8.77	8.38
2008	CVX	91.00	2.46	2.70%	73.97	-16.01%	2,514	2,770	11.67	7.80
2009	CVX	73.97	2.66	3.60%	76.99	7.68%	2,707	3,067	5.24	14.12
2010	CVX	76.99	2.80	3.64%	91.25	22.16%	3,307	3,395	9.53	8.08
2011	CVX	91.25	3.06	3.35%	106.40	19.96%	3,967	3,760	13.44	6.79
2012	CVX	106.40	3.51	3.30%	108.14	4.93%	4,163	4,163		
				DIA	SPY	XLE	2012	Cumul	Fiscal yr end	
			Cumulative	10.68%	8.69%	-2.15%	39.06%	5 yr	31-Dec	
			Cumulative	94.13%	95.71%	270.76%	340.31%	10 yr		
			Cumulative	90.91%	46.69%	283.04%	316.30%	14 yr		

Spreadsheet 6.7 ConnocoPhillips

Year Ending 31-Dec	Sym	XLE Begin Price	Div	S&P Energy ETF Div Pct	End Price	Gain Loss	$ Value	Yearly Ave Tot Ret 12.42%	EPS	Year End P/E
1998	COP				21.31		1,000	1,000		
1999	COP	21.31	0.68	3.19%	23.50	13.45%	1,135	1,124		
2000	COP	23.50	0.68	2.89%	28.44	23.90%	1,406	1,264	3.60	6.53
2001	COP	28.44	0.70	2.46%	30.13	8.41%	1,524	1,421	2.71	10.49
2002	COP	30.13	0.74	2.46%	24.20	-17.24%	1,261	1,597	0.72	41.85
2003	COP	24.20	0.82	3.37%	32.79	38.87%	1,752	1,795	3.35	7.22
2004	COP	32.79	0.90	2.73%	43.42	35.15%	2,367	2,018	5.79	5.66
2005	COP	43.42	1.06	2.44%	58.18	36.45%	3,230	2,269	9.63	4.51
2006	COP	58.18	1.44	2.48%	71.95	26.14%	4,075	2,550	9.66	6.02
2007	COP	71.95	1.64	2.28%	88.30	25.00%	5,093	2,867	7.22	9.97
2008	COP	88.30	1.88	2.13%	51.80	-39.21%	3,096	3,223	(11.16)	
2009	COP	51.80	1.91	3.69%	51.07	2.28%	3,167	3,623	3.24	15.99
2010	COP	51.07	2.15	4.21%	68.10	37.56%	4,356	4,073	6.71	7.61
2011	COP	68.10	2.64	3.88%	72.87	10.88%	4,830	4,578	8.97	7.59
2012	COP	72.87	19.67	26.99%	57.99	6.57%	5,147	5,147		
Includes asset sale in 2012				DIA	SPY	XLE	2012	Cumul	Fiscal yr end	
			Cumulative	10.68%	8.69%	-2.15%	1.06%	5 yr	31-Dec	
			Cumulative	94.13%	95.71%	270.76%	308.12%	10 yr		
			Cumulative	90.91%	46.69%	283.04%	414.75%	14 yr		

Spreadsheet 6.8 Royal Dutch Shell

Year Ending 31-Dec	Sym	XLE Begin Price	Div	S&P Energy ETF Div Pct	End Price	Gain Loss	$ Value	Yearly Ave Tot Ret 6.17%	EPS	Year End P/E
2005	RDS-B				64.53		1,000	1,000		
2006	RDS-B	64.53	2.54	3.94%	71.15	14.20%	1,142	1,062	3.95	16.34
2007	RDS-B	71.15	2.88	4.05%	83.00	20.70%	1,378	1,127	4.99	14.26
2008	RDS-B	83.00	3.20	3.86%	51.43	-34.18%	907	1,197	4.26	19.48
2009	RDS-B	51.43	3.36	6.53%	58.13	19.56%	1,085	1,271	2.04	25.21
2010	RDS-B	58.13	3.36	5.78%	66.67	20.47%	1,307	1,349	3.28	17.72
2011	RDS-B	66.67	3.36	5.04%	76.01	19.05%	1,556	1,432	4.97	13.41
2012	RDS-B	76.01	3.42	4.50%	70.89	-2.24%	1,521	1,521	4.24	17.93
				DIA	SPY	XLE	2012	Cumul	Fiscal yr end	
			Cumulative	10.68%	8.69%	-2.15%	10.34%	5 yr	31-Dec	
			Cumulative	94.13%	95.71%	270.76%		10 yr		
			Cumulative	90.91%	46.69%	283.04%		14 yr		

Spreadsheet 6.9 Realty Income

Year Ending 31-Dec	XLF Sym	S&P Financial ETF Begin Price	Div	Div Pct	End Price	Gain Loss	$ Value	Yearly Ave Tot Ret 16.58%	Year End EPS	P/E
1998	O				11.16		1,000	1,000		
1999	O	11.16	1.04	9.34%	10.14	0.20%	1,002	1,166	0.77	14.49
2000	O	10.14	1.09	10.76%	12.44	33.44%	1,337	1,359	0.81	12.52
2001	O	12.44	1.12	9.01%	14.70	27.18%	1,701	1,584	0.91	13.67
2002	O	14.70	1.16	7.87%	17.50	26.92%	2,158	1,847	0.82	17.93
2003	O	17.50	1.18	6.75%	20.00	21.04%	2,612	2,153	0.86	20.35
2004	O	20.00	1.24	6.21%	25.29	32.66%	3,465	2,510	0.87	22.99
2005	O	25.29	1.35	5.32%	21.62	-9.19%	3,147	2,926	0.98	25.81
2006	O	21.62	1.44	6.65%	27.70	34.77%	4,241	3,411	1.03	20.99
2007	O	27.70	1.56	5.63%	27.02	3.17%	4,376	3,977	1.01	27.43
2008	O	27.02	1.66	6.15%	23.15	-8.17%	4,018	4,636	0.91	29.69
2009	O	23.15	1.71	7.37%	25.91	19.29%	4,793	5,404	0.94	24.63
2010	O	25.91	1.72	6.64%	34.20	38.64%	6,646	6,300	0.93	27.86
2011	O	34.20	1.74	5.08%	34.96	7.30%	7,131	7,345	1.01	33.86
2012	O	34.96	1.77	5.06%	40.21	20.08%	8,562	8,562		
				DIA	SPY	XLF	2012	Cumul	Fiscal yr end	
		Cumulative		10.68%	8.69%	-36.11%	95.68%	5 yr	31-Dec	
		Cumulative		94.13%	95.71%	-6.01%	296.72%	10 yr		
		Cumulative		90.91%	46.69%	-6.33%	756.24%	14 yr		

Spreadsheet 6.10 Health Care REIT

Year Ending 31-Dec	XLF Sym	S&P Financial ETF Begin Price	Div	Div Pct	End Price	Gain Loss	$ Value	Yearly Ave Tot Ret 14.43%	Year End EPS	P/E
1998	HCN				25.88		1,000	1,000		
1999	HCN	25.88	2.27	8.77%	15.13	-32.77%	672	1,144	2.21	11.71
2000	HCN	15.13	2.34	15.43%	16.25	22.84%	826	1,309	1.76	8.60
2001	HCN	16.25	2.34	14.40%	24.35	64.25%	1,356	1,498	1.36	11.95
2002	HCN	24.35	2.34	9.61%	27.05	20.70%	1,637	1,715	1.31	18.59
2003	HCN	27.05	2.34	8.65%	36.00	41.74%	2,321	1,962	1.35	20.04
2004	HCN	36.00	2.39	6.63%	38.15	12.60%	2,613	2,245	1.33	27.07
2005	HCN	38.15	2.46	6.45%	33.90	-4.69%	2,490	2,569	1.02	37.40
2006	HCN	33.90	2.54	7.49%	43.02	34.40%	3,347	2,940	1.10	30.82
2007	HCN	43.02	2.28	5.30%	44.69	9.18%	3,654	3,364	0.68	63.26
2008	HCN	44.69	2.70	6.04%	42.20	0.47%	3,671	3,849	0.91	49.11
2009	HCN	42.20	2.72	6.45%	44.32	11.47%	4,092	4,405	0.90	46.89
2010	HCN	44.32	2.74	6.18%	47.64	13.67%	4,652	5,041	0.30	147.73
2011	HCN	47.64	2.84	5.95%	54.53	20.41%	5,601	5,768	0.48	99.25
2012	HCN	54.53	2.96	5.43%	61.29	17.83%	6,600	6,600		
				DIA	SPY	XLF	2012	Cumul	Fiscal yr end	
		Cumulative		10.68%	8.69%	-36.11%	80.62%	5 yr	31-Dec	
		Cumulative		94.13%	95.71%	-6.01%	303.11%	10 yr		
		Cumulative		90.91%	46.69%	-6.33%	559.98%	14 yr		

Spreadsheet 6.11 Wells Fargo

Year Ending 31-Dec	Sym	XLF Begin Price	Div	S&P Financial ETF Div Pct	End Price	Gain Loss	$ Value	Yearly Ave Tot Ret 8.47%	Year End EPS	P/E
1998	WFC				15.47		1,000	1,000		
1999	WFC	15.47	0.39	2.54%	20.22	33.24%	1,332	1,085		
2000	WFC	20.22	0.45	2.23%	27.85	39.94%	1,865	1,177		
2001	WFC	27.85	0.50	1.80%	21.74	-20.15%	1,489	1,276		
2002	WFC	21.74	0.55	2.53%	23.44	10.35%	1,643	1,384	1.66	13.09
2003	WFC	23.44	0.75	3.20%	29.45	28.85%	2,117	1,502	1.83	12.81
2004	WFC	29.45	0.93	3.16%	31.08	8.69%	2,301	1,629	2.05	14.36
2005	WFC	31.08	1.00	3.22%	31.42	4.31%	2,400	1,767	2.25	13.81
2006	WFC	31.42	1.08	3.44%	35.56	16.63%	2,799	1,917	2.47	12.72
2007	WFC	35.56	1.18	3.32%	30.19	-11.78%	2,470	2,079	2.38	14.94
2008	WFC	30.19	1.30	4.31%	29.48	1.95%	2,518	2,255	0.70	43.13
2009	WFC	29.48	0.49	1.66%	26.99	-6.78%	2,347	2,446	1.75	16.85
2010	WFC	26.99	0.20	0.74%	30.99	15.56%	2,712	2,653	2.21	12.21
2011	WFC	30.99	0.48	1.55%	27.56	-9.52%	2,454	2,878	2.82	10.99
2012	WFC	27.56	0.88	3.19%	34.18	27.21%	3,122	3,122		
				DIA	SPY	XLF	2012	Cumul	Fiscal yr end	
			Cumulative	10.68%	8.69%	-36.11%	26.41%	5 yr	31-Dec	
			Cumulative	94.13%	95.71%	-6.01%	90.01%	10 yr		
			Cumulative	90.91%	46.69%	-6.33%	212.19%	14 yr		

Spreadsheet 6.12 BB&T Bank

Year Ending 31-Dec	Sym	XLF Begin Price	Div	S&P Financial ETF Div Pct	End Price	Gain Loss	Value	Yearly Ave Tot Ret 1.33%	Year End EPS	P/E
1998	BBT				39.16		1,000	1,000		
1999	BBT	39.16	0.75	1.92%	27.16	-28.73%	713	1,013		
2000	BBT	27.16	0.86	3.17%	37.31	40.54%	1,002	1,027	1.53	17.75
2001	BBT	37.31	0.98	2.63%	36.11	-0.59%	996	1,041	2.12	17.60
2002	BBT	36.11	1.10	3.05%	36.99	5.48%	1,050	1,054	2.70	13.37
2003	BBT	36.99	1.22	3.30%	38.64	7.76%	1,132	1,069	2.07	17.87
2004	BBT	38.64	1.34	3.47%	42.05	12.29%	1,271	1,083	2.80	13.80
2005	BBT	42.05	1.46	3.47%	41.91	3.14%	1,311	1,097	3.00	14.02
2006	BBT	41.91	1.60	3.82%	43.93	8.64%	1,424	1,112	2.81	14.91
2007	BBT	43.93	1.76	4.01%	30.67	-26.18%	1,051	1,127	3.14	13.99
2008	BBT	30.67	1.86	6.06%	27.46	-4.40%	1,005	1,142	2.71	11.32
2009	BBT	27.46	1.24	4.52%	25.37	-3.10%	974	1,157	1.15	23.88
2010	BBT	25.37	0.60	2.36%	26.29	5.99%	1,032	1,172	1.27	19.98
2011	BBT	26.29	0.64	2.43%	25.17	-1.83%	1,013	1,188	1.83	14.37
2012	BBT	25.17	0.80	3.18%	29.11	18.83%	1,204	1,204		
				DIA	SPY	XLF	2012	Cumul	Fiscal yr end	
			Cumulative	10.68%	8.69%	-36.11%	14.55%	5 yr	31-Dec	
			Cumulative	94.13%	95.71%	-6.01%	14.65%	10 yr		
			Cumulative	90.91%	46.69%	-6.33%	20.42%	14 yr		

Spreadsheet 6.13 Citigroup

Year Ending 31-Dec	Sym	XLF Begin Price	Div	S&P Financial ETF Div Pct	End Price	Gain Loss	Value	Yearly Ave Tot Ret -9.29%	Year End EPS	P/E
1998	C				49.69		1,000	1,000		
1999	C	33.09	0.54	1.63%	55.69	69.91%	1,699	907		
2000	C	41.77	0.52	1.24%	51.06	23.49%	2,098	823	2.36	17.70
2001	C	51.06	0.60	1.18%	50.48	0.04%	2,099	747	2.55	20.02
2002	C	50.48	3.12	6.17%	35.19	-24.12%	1,593	677	2.59	19.49
2003	C	35.19	1.10	3.13%	48.54	41.06%	2,247	614	3.27	10.76
2004	C	48.54	1.60	3.30%	48.18	2.55%	2,304	557	3.07	15.81
2005	C	48.18	1.76	3.65%	48.53	4.38%	2,405	506	3.82	12.61
2006	C	48.53	1.96	4.04%	55.70	18.81%	2,858	459	4.09	11.87
2007	C	55.70	2.16	3.88%	29.44	-43.27%	1,621	416	0.59	94.41
2008	C	29.44	1.12	3.80%	6.71	-73.40%	431	377	(6.35)	
2009	C	6.71	0.01	0.15%	3.31	-50.52%	213	342	(0.76)	
2010	C	3.31	0.00	0.00%	4.73	42.90%	305	311	0.37	8.95
2011	C	47.30	0.03	0.06%	26.31	-44.31%	170	282	3.66	12.92
2012	C	26.31	0.04	0.15%	39.56	50.51%	256	256		
				DIA	SPY	XLF	2012	Cumul	Fiscal yr end	
			Cumulative	10.68%	8.69%	-36.11%	-84.24%	5 yr	31-Dec	
			Cumulative	94.13%	95.71%	-6.01%	-83.96%	10 yr		
			Cumulative	90.91%	46.69%	-6.33%	-74.45%	14 yr		

Spreadsheet 6.14 General Electric

Year Ending 31-Dec	Sym	XLI Begin Price	Div	Industrial Div Pct	End Price	Gain Loss	Value	Yearly Ave Tot Ret -0.62%	Year End EPS	P/E
1998	GE				102.00		1,000	1,000		
1999	GE	102.00	1.46	1.43%	154.75	53.15%	1,531	994	1.07	31.74
2000	GE	51.58	0.57	1.11%	47.94	-5.96%	1,440	988	1.27	40.62
2001	GE	47.94	0.61	1.27%	40.08	-15.13%	1,222	982	1.41	34.00
2002	GE	40.08	0.73	1.82%	24.35	-37.43%	765	975	1.52	26.37
2003	GE	24.35	0.77	3.16%	30.98	30.39%	997	969	1.40	17.39
2004	GE	30.98	0.82	2.65%	36.50	20.46%	1,201	963	1.59	19.48
2005	GE	36.50	0.91	2.49%	35.05	-1.48%	1,184	957	1.64	22.26
2006	GE	35.05	1.03	2.94%	37.21	9.10%	1,291	951	1.86	18.84
2007	GE	37.21	1.15	3.09%	37.07	2.71%	1,326	946	2.20	16.91
2008	GE	37.07	1.24	3.35%	16.20	-52.95%	624	940	1.78	20.83
2009	GE	16.20	0.61	3.77%	15.13	-2.84%	606	934	0.73	22.19
2010	GE	15.13	0.42	2.78%	18.29	23.66%	750	928	1.19	12.71
2011	GE	18.29	0.58	3.17%	17.91	1.09%	758	922	1.23	14.87
2012	GE	17.91	0.68	3.80%	20.99	20.99%	917	917		
				DIA	SPY	XLI	2012	Cumul	Fiscal yr end	
			Cumulative	10.68%	8.69%	8.61%	-30.86%	5 yr	31-Dec	
			Cumulative	94.13%	95.71%	122.15%	19.90%	10 yr		
			Cumulative	90.91%	46.69%	98.08%	-8.29%	14 yr		

Spreadsheet 6.15 United Parcel Service

Year Ending 31-Dec	Sym	XLI Industrial Begin Price	Div	Div Pct	End Price	Gain Loss	Value	Yearly Ave Tot Ret 2.63%	Year End EPS	P/E
1999	UPS						1,000	1,000		
2000	UPS	69.00	0.68	0.99%	58.75	-13.87%	861	1,026	2.50	27.60
2001	UPS	58.75	0.76	1.29%	54.50	-5.94%	810	1,053	2.12	27.71
2002	UPS	54.50	0.76	1.39%	63.08	17.14%	949	1,081	2.87	18.99
2003	UPS	63.08	0.92	1.46%	74.55	19.64%	1,135	1,109	2.55	24.74
2004	UPS	74.55	1.12	1.50%	85.46	16.14%	1,319	1,139	2.93	25.44
2005	UPS	85.46	1.32	1.54%	75.15	-10.52%	1,180	1,169	3.47	24.63
2006	UPS	75.15	1.52	2.02%	74.98	1.80%	1,201	1,199	3.86	19.47
2007	UPS	74.98	1.68	2.24%	70.72	-3.44%	1,160	1,231	0.36	208.28
2008	UPS	70.72	1.80	2.55%	55.16	-19.46%	934	1,263	2.94	24.05
2009	UPS	55.16	1.80	3.26%	57.37	7.27%	1,002	1,296	2.14	25.78
2010	UPS	57.37	1.88	3.28%	72.58	29.79%	1,300	1,331	3.56	16.12
2011	UPS	72.58	2.08	2.87%	73.19	3.71%	1,349	1,366	4.25	17.08
2012	UPS	73.19	2.28	3.12%	73.73	3.85%	1,401	1,401		
				DIA	SPY	XLI	2012	Cumul	Fiscal yr end	
			Cumulative	10.68%	8.69%	8.61%	20.77%	5 yr	31-Dec	
			Cumulative	94.13%	95.71%	122.15%	47.60%	10 yr		
			Cumulative	90.91%	46.69%	98.08%		14 yr		

Spreadsheet 6.16 Emerson Electric

Year Ending 31-Dec	Sym	XLI Industrial Begin Price	Div	Div Pct	End Price	Gain Loss	Value	Yearly Ave Tot Ret 6.99%	Year End EPS	P/E
1998	EMR				58.76		1,000	1,000		
1999	EMR	58.76	1.333	2.27%	56.95	-0.81%	992	1,070		
2000	EMR	56.95	1.455	2.55%	78.81	40.94%	1,398	1,145	1.65	34.52
2001	EMR	78.81	1.535	1.95%	57.10	-25.60%	1,040	1,225	1.22	64.60
2002	EMR	57.10	1.555	2.72%	50.85	-8.22%	955	1,310	1.28	44.61
2003	EMR	50.85	1.578	3.10%	64.75	30.44%	1,245	1,402	1.20	42.38
2004	EMR	64.75	1.615	2.49%	70.10	10.76%	1,379	1,500	1.49	43.46
2005	EMR	70.10	1.690	2.41%	67.95	-0.66%	1,370	1,605	1.70	41.24
2006	EMR	33.98	0.930	2.74%	44.09	32.51%	1,815	1,717	2.20	15.44
2007	EMR	44.09	1.088	2.47%	56.66	30.98%	2,378	1,837	2.62	16.83
2008	EMR	56.66	1.230	2.17%	36.61	-33.22%	1,588	1,965	3.08	18.40
2009	EMR	36.61	1.325	3.62%	42.60	19.98%	1,905	2,103	2.24	16.34
2010	EMR	42.60	1.350	3.17%	57.17	37.37%	2,617	2,250	2.60	16.38
2011	EMR	57.17	1.435	2.51%	46.59	-16.00%	2,199	2,407	3.26	17.54
2012	EMR	46.59	1.610	3.46%	52.96	17.13%	2,575	2,575		
				DIA	SPY	XLI	2012	Cumul	Fiscal yr end	
			Cumulative	10.68%	8.69%	8.61%	8.30%	5 yr	30-Sep	
			Cumulative	94.13%	95.71%	122.15%	169.77%	10 yr		
			Cumulative	90.91%	46.69%	98.08%	157.51%	14 yr		

Spreadsheet 6.17 R P M International

Year Ending 31-Dec	Sym	XLB Begin Price	Div	S&P 400 Div Pct	Materials End Price	Gain Loss	Value	Yearly Ave Tot Ret 8.41%	Year End EPS	P/E
1998	RPM				16.00		1,000	1,000		
1999	RPM	16.00	0.48	2.97%	10.19	-33.34%	667	1,084		
2000	RPM	10.19	0.49	4.83%	8.56	-11.16%	592	1,175		
2001	RPM	8.56	0.50	5.84%	14.46	74.77%	1,035	1,274		
2002	RPM	14.46	0.51	3.49%	15.28	9.16%	1,130	1,381	0.97	14.91
2003	RPM	15.28	0.53	3.47%	16.46	11.19%	1,256	1,497	0.30	50.93
2004	RPM	16.46	0.57	3.46%	19.66	22.90%	1,544	1,623	1.16	14.19
2005	RPM	19.66	0.61	3.10%	17.37	-8.55%	1,412	1,760	0.86	22.86
2006	RPM	17.37	0.66	3.77%	20.89	24.04%	1,751	1,908	(0.65)	
2007	RPM	20.89	0.72	3.42%	20.30	0.60%	1,762	2,068	1.64	12.74
2008	RPM	20.30	0.77	3.79%	13.29	-30.74%	1,220	2,242	0.36	56.39
2009	RPM	13.29	0.81	6.06%	20.33	59.03%	1,941	2,431	0.93	14.29
2010	RPM	20.33	0.83	4.08%	22.10	12.79%	2,189	2,635	1.39	14.63
2011	RPM	22.10	0.85	3.82%	24.55	14.91%	2,515	2,857	1.45	15.24
2012	RPM	24.55	0.87	3.54%	29.36	23.14%	3,097	3,097		
				DIA	SPY	XLB	2012	Cumul	Fiscal yr end	
			Cumulative	10.68%	8.69%	2.20%	75.78%	5 yr	31-May	
			Cumulative	94.13%	95.71%	137.56%	174.13%	10 yr		
			Cumulative	90.91%	46.69%	137.41%	209.69%	14 yr		

Spreadsheet 6.18 Air Products & Chemicals

Year Ending 31-Dec	Sym	XLB Begin Price	Div	Materials Div Pct	End Price	Gain Loss	Value	Yearly Ave Tot Ret 7.74%	Year End EPS	P/E
1998	APD				40.00		1,000	1,000		
1999	APD	40.00	0.71	1.78%	33.56	-14.33%	857	1,077		
2000	APD	33.56	0.75	2.23%	41.00	24.40%	1,066	1,161		
2001	APD	41.00	0.79	1.93%	46.91	16.34%	1,240	1,250		
2002	APD	46.91	0.83	1.77%	42.75	-7.10%	1,152	1,347	2.36	19.88
2003	APD	42.75	0.90	2.11%	52.83	25.68%	1,448	1,451	1.79	23.88
2004	APD	52.83	1.10	2.08%	57.97	11.81%	1,619	1,564	2.66	19.86
2005	APD	57.97	1.28	2.21%	59.19	4.31%	1,689	1,685	3.04	19.07
2006	APD	59.19	1.36	2.30%	70.28	21.03%	2,044	1,815	3.23	18.33
2007	APD	70.28	1.52	2.16%	98.83	42.79%	2,918	1,955	4.57	15.38
2008	APD	98.83	1.76	1.78%	50.27	-47.35%	1,536	2,107	4.97	19.89
2009	APD	50.27	1.80	3.58%	81.06	64.83%	2,532	2,269	3.00	16.76
2010	APD	81.06	1.96	2.42%	90.95	14.62%	2,903	2,445	4.74	17.10
2011	APD	90.95	2.32	2.55%	85.19	-3.78%	2,793	2,634	5.59	16.27
2012	APD	85.19	2.56	3.01%	84.02	1.63%	2,838	2,838		
				DIA	SPY	XLB	2012	Cumul	Fiscal yr end	
			Cumulative	10.68%	8.69%	2.20%	-2.74%	5 yr	30-Sep	
			Cumulative	94.13%	95.71%	137.56%	146.40%	10 yr		
			Cumulative	90.91%	46.69%	137.41%	183.85%	14 yr		

Spreadsheet 6.19 DuPont XLB Materials

Year Ending 31-Dec	Sym	Begin Price	Div	Div Pct	End Price	Gain Loss	Value	Yearly Ave Tot Ret 2.31%	Year End EPS	P/E
1998	DD				53.06		1,000	1,000		
1999	DD	53.06	1.40	2.64%	65.87	26.78%	1,268	1,023		
2000	DD	65.87	1.40	2.13%	48.31	-24.53%	957	1,047		
2001	DD	48.31	1.40	2.90%	42.51	-9.11%	870	1,071		
2002	DD	42.51	1.40	3.29%	42.40	3.03%	896	1,096	1.83	23.23
2003	DD	42.40	1.40	3.30%	45.89	11.53%	999	1,121	0.99	42.83
2004	DD	45.89	1.40	3.05%	49.05	9.94%	1,099	1,147	1.76	26.07
2005	DD	49.05	1.46	2.98%	42.50	-10.38%	985	1,173	2.07	23.70
2006	DD	42.50	1.48	3.48%	48.71	18.09%	1,163	1,200	3.38	12.57
2007	DD	48.71	1.52	3.12%	44.09	-6.36%	1,089	1,228	3.22	15.13
2008	DD	44.09	1.64	3.72%	25.30	-38.90%	665	1,257	2.20	20.04
2009	DD	25.30	1.64	6.48%	33.67	39.57%	929	1,286	1.92	13.18
2010	DD	33.67	1.64	4.87%	49.88	53.01%	1,421	1,315	3.28	10.27
2011	DD	49.88	1.64	3.29%	45.78	-4.93%	1,351	1,346	3.68	13.55
2012	DD	45.78	1.70	3.71%	44.98	1.97%	1,377	1,377		
				DIA	SPY	XLB	2012	Cumul	Fiscal yr end	
			Cumulative	10.68%	8.69%	2.20%	26.49%	5 yr	31-Dec	
			Cumulative	94.13%	95.71%	137.56%	53.71%	10 yr		
			Cumulative	90.91%	46.69%	137.41%	37.72%	14 yr		

Spreadsheet 6.20 Intel XLK Technology

Year Ending 31-Dec	Sym	Begin Price	Div	Div Pct	End Price	Gain Loss	Value	Yearly Ave Tot Ret -0.90%	Year End EPS	P/E
1998	INTC				29.64		1,000	1,000		
1999	INTC	29.64	0.06	0.19%	41.16	39.05%	1,391	991		
2000	INTC	41.16	0.07	0.17%	30.06	-26.80%	1,018	982	1.51	27.26
2001	INTC	30.06	0.08	0.27%	31.45	4.89%	1,068	973	0.19	158.21
2002	INTC	31.45	0.08	0.25%	15.57	-50.24%	531	964	0.46	68.37
2003	INTC	15.57	0.08	0.51%	32.05	106.36%	1,096	956	0.85	18.32
2004	INTC	32.05	0.16	0.50%	23.39	-26.52%	806	947	1.16	27.63
2005	INTC	23.39	0.32	1.37%	24.96	8.08%	871	939	1.40	16.71
2006	INTC	24.96	0.40	1.60%	20.25	-17.27%	720	930	0.95	26.27
2007	INTC	20.25	0.45	2.22%	26.66	33.88%	964	922	1.29	15.70
2008	INTC	26.66	0.55	2.05%	14.66	-42.96%	550	914	1.21	22.03
2009	INTC	14.66	0.56	3.82%	20.40	42.97%	786	905	1.19	12.32
2010	INTC	20.40	0.63	3.09%	21.03	6.18%	835	897	2.01	10.15
2011	INTC	21.03	0.78	3.72%	24.25	19.03%	994	889	2.39	8.80
2012	INTC	24.25	0.87	3.59%	20.62	-11.38%	881	881		
				DIA	SPY	XLK	2012	Cumul	Fiscal yr end	
			Cumulative	10.68%	8.69%	16.31%	-8.66%	5 yr	31-Dec	
			Cumulative	94.13%	95.71%	119.74%	65.80%	10 yr		
			Cumulative	90.91%	46.69%	-0.02%	-11.91%	14 yr		

Spreadsheet 6.21 Verizon

Year Ending 31-Dec	X L K Sym	Begin Price	Div	Div Pct	End Price	Gain Loss	Value	Yearly Ave Tot Ret 4.10%	E P S	P / E
2000	VZ				48.08		1,000	1,000		
2001	VZ	48.08	1.54	3.20%	45.53	-2.10%	979	1,041	0.21	228.95
2002	VZ	45.53	1.54	3.38%	37.17	-14.98%	832	1,084	1.67	27.26
2003	VZ	37.17	1.54	4.14%	33.65	-5.33%	788	1,128	1.25	29.74
2004	VZ	33.65	1.54	4.58%	38.86	20.06%	946	1,174	2.11	15.95
2005	VZ	38.86	1.62	4.17%	28.89	-21.49%	743	1,223	2.16	17.99
2006	VZ	28.89	1.62	5.61%	37.07	33.92%	995	1,273	1.88	15.37
2007	VZ	37.07	1.67	4.50%	43.49	21.82%	1,212	1,325	2.23	16.62
2008	VZ	43.49	1.78	4.09%	33.90	-17.96%	994	1,379	2.87	15.15
2009	VZ	33.90	1.87	5.52%	33.13	3.24%	1,026	1,436	1.72	19.71
2010	VZ	33.13	3.52	10.63%	35.78	18.63%	1,218	1,495	0.90	36.81
2011	VZ	35.78	1.96	5.48%	40.12	17.61%	1,432	1,556	0.85	42.09
2012	VZ	40.12	2.02	5.02%	43.37	13.12%	1,620	1,620	2.50	16.05
				DIA	SPY	XLK	2012	Cumul	Fiscal yr end	
			Cumulative	10.68%	8.69%	16.31%	33.69%	5 yr	31-Dec	
			Cumulative	94.13%	95.71%	119.74%	94.65%	10 yr		
			Cumulative	90.91%	46.69%	-0.02%		14 yr		

Spreadsheet 6.22 AT&T

Year Ending 31-Dec	X L K Sym	Begin Price	Div	Div Pct	End Price	Gain Loss	Value	Yearly Ave Tot Ret 0.97%	Year End E P S	P / E
1998	T				53.63		1,000	1,000		
1999	T	53.63	0.96	1.78%	48.75	-7.32%	927	1,010		
2000	T	48.75	1.01	2.06%	47.75	0.01%	927	1,019		
2001	T	47.75	1.02	2.14%	39.17	-15.83%	780	1,029		
2002	T	39.17	1.07	2.72%	27.11	-28.07%	561	1,039	2.20	8.90
2003	T	27.11	1.42	5.23%	26.07	1.39%	569	1,049	1.76	15.40
2004	T	26.07	1.25	4.79%	25.77	3.64%	590	1,060	1.50	17.38
2005	T	25.77	1.29	5.01%	24.49	0.04%	590	1,070	1.42	18.15
2006	T	24.49	1.33	5.43%	35.75	51.41%	893	1,080	1.89	12.96
2007	T	35.75	1.42	3.97%	41.56	20.22%	1,074	1,091	1.94	18.43
2008	T	41.56	1.60	3.85%	28.50	-27.57%	778	1,101	(0.44)	
2009	T	28.50	1.64	5.75%	28.03	4.11%	810	1,112	2.05	13.90
2010	T	28.03	1.68	5.99%	29.38	10.81%	897	1,123	3.22	8.70
2011	T	29.38	1.72	5.85%	30.24	8.78%	976	1,134	0.66	44.52
2012	T	30.24	1.76	5.82%	33.71	17.29%	1,145	1,145		
				DIA	SPY	XLK	2012	Cumul	Fiscal yr end	
			Cumulative	10.68%	8.69%	16.31%	6.60%	5 yr	31-Dec	
			Cumulative	94.13%	95.71%	119.74%	104.00%	10 yr		
			Cumulative	90.91%	46.69%	-0.02%	14.49%	14 yr		

Spreadsheet 6.23 Johnson & Johnson XLV Health Care- Pharma

Year Ending 31-Dec	Sym	Begin Price	Div	Div Pct	End Price	Gain Loss	Value	Yearly Ave Tot Ret 6.07%	Year End EPS	P/E
1998	JNJ				83.87		1,000	1,000		
1999	JNJ	83.87	1.09	1.30%	93.25	12.48%	1,125	1,061		
2000	JNJ	93.25	1.24	1.33%	105.06	13.99%	1,282	1,125	1.61	28.96
2001	JNJ	52.53	0.70	1.33%	59.10	13.84%	1,460	1,194	1.84	28.55
2002	JNJ	59.10	0.80	1.35%	53.71	-7.77%	1,346	1,266	2.16	27.36
2003	JNJ	53.71	0.93	1.72%	51.66	-2.09%	1,318	1,343	2.40	22.38
2004	JNJ	51.66	1.10	2.12%	63.42	24.88%	1,646	1,424	2.74	18.85
2005	JNJ	63.42	1.28	2.01%	60.10	-3.22%	1,593	1,511	3.35	18.93
2006	JNJ	60.10	1.46	2.42%	66.02	12.27%	1,788	1,603	3.73	16.11
2007	JNJ	66.02	1.62	2.45%	66.70	3.48%	1,851	1,700	3.63	18.19
2008	JNJ	66.70	1.80	2.69%	59.83	-7.61%	1,710	1,803	4.57	14.60
2009	JNJ	59.83	1.93	3.23%	64.41	10.88%	1,896	1,913	4.40	13.60
2010	JNJ	64.41	2.11	3.28%	61.85	-0.70%	1,883	2,029	4.78	13.47
2011	JNJ	61.85	2.25	3.64%	65.58	9.67%	2,065	2,152	3.49	17.72
2012	JNJ	65.58	2.40	3.66%	70.10	10.55%	2,283	2,283		
				DIA	SPY	XLV	2012	Cumul	Fiscal yr end	
			Cumulative	10.68%	8.69%	24.41%	23.34%	5 yr	31-Dec	
			Cumulative	94.13%	95.71%	76.36%	69.55%	10 yr		
			Cumulative	90.91%	46.69%	83.34%	128.26%	14 yr		

Spreadsheet 6.24 Abbott Labs XLV Health Care- Pharma

Year Ending 31-Dec	Sym	Begin Price	Div	Div Pct	End Price	Gain Loss	Value	Yearly Ave Tot Ret 5.53%	Year End EPS	P/E
1998	ABT				45.99		1,000	1,000		
1999	ABT	45.99	0.66	1.44%	34.19	-24.22%	758	1,055		
2000	ABT	34.19	0.74	2.16%	45.52	35.30%	1,025	1,114	1.78	19.21
2001	ABT	45.52	0.82	1.80%	52.39	16.89%	1,198	1,175	0.99	45.98
2002	ABT	52.39	0.92	1.75%	37.59	-26.50%	881	1,240	1.62	32.34
2003	ABT	37.59	0.97	2.58%	43.79	19.07%	1,049	1,309	1.59	23.64
2004	ABT	43.79	3.87	8.84%	46.92	15.99%	1,217	1,381	2.02	21.68
2005	ABT	46.92	1.09	2.31%	39.43	-13.65%	1,050	1,458	2.44	19.23
2006	ABT	39.43	1.16	2.94%	48.71	26.48%	1,329	1,538	2.42	16.29
2007	ABT	48.71	1.27	2.61%	56.15	17.88%	1,566	1,624	2.31	21.09
2008	ABT	56.15	1.31	2.32%	53.37	-2.63%	1,525	1,713	3.03	18.53
2009	ABT	53.37	1.56	2.92%	53.99	4.08%	1,587	1,808	3.69	14.46
2010	ABT	53.99	1.72	3.19%	47.91	-8.08%	1,459	1,908	3.00	18.00
2011	ABT	47.91	1.88	3.92%	56.23	21.29%	1,770	2,014	3.04	15.76
2012	ABT	56.23	2.01	3.57%	65.50	20.06%	2,125	2,125		
				DIA	SPY	XLV	2012	Cumul	Fiscal yr end	
			Cumulative	10.68%	8.69%	24.41%	35.67%	5 yr	31-Dec	
			Cumulative	94.13%	95.71%	76.36%	141.23%	10 yr		
			Cumulative	90.91%	46.69%	83.34%	112.49%	14 yr		

Spreadsheet 6.25 Southern Company

Year Ending 31-Dec	Sym	XLU Utilities-Electricity Begin Price	Div	Div Pct	End Price	Gain Loss	Value	Yearly Ave Tot Ret 11.32%	Year End EPS	P/E
1998	SO				27.27		1,000	1,000		
1999	SO	27.27	1.36	4.99%	23.19	-9.97%	900	1,113		
2000	SO	23.19	1.36	5.86%	33.25	49.25%	1,344	1,239	2.01	16.54
2001	SO	33.25	15.16	45.59%	25.35	21.83%	1,637	1,380	1.82	13.93
2002	SO	25.35	1.36	5.36%	28.39	17.36%	1,921	1,536	1.85	15.35
2003	SO	28.39	1.38	4.86%	30.25	11.41%	2,140	1,710	2.02	14.98
2004	SO	30.25	1.42	4.71%	33.52	15.52%	2,472	1,903	2.06	16.27
2005	SO	33.52	1.48	4.40%	34.53	7.41%	2,656	2,119	2.13	16.21
2006	SO	34.53	1.54	4.45%	36.86	11.20%	2,953	2,359	2.13	17.31
2007	SO	36.86	1.60	4.33%	38.75	9.45%	3,232	2,626	2.29	16.92
2008	SO	38.75	1.66	4.29%	37.00	-0.23%	3,225	2,923	2.26	16.37
2009	SO	37.00	1.73	4.68%	33.32	-5.26%	3,055	3,254	2.06	16.17
2010	SO	33.32	1.82	5.46%	38.23	20.20%	3,672	3,622	2.36	16.20
2011	SO	38.23	1.87	4.90%	42.37	15.73%	4,250	4,032	2.57	16.49
2012	SO	42.37	1.94	4.58%	42.81	5.62%	4,489	4,489		

		DIA	SPY	XLU	2012	Cumul	Fiscal yr end
	Cumulative	10.68%	8.69%	0.66%	38.88%	5 yr	31-Dec
	Cumulative	94.13%	95.71%	158.75%	133.67%	10 yr	
	Cumulative	90.91%	46.69%	89.63%	348.91%	14 yr	

Spreadsheet 6.26 Oneok

Year Ending 31-Dec	Sym	XLU Utilities-Gas Begin Price	Div	Div Pct	End Price	Gain Loss	Value	Yearly Ave Tot Ret 16.04%	Year End EPS	P/E
1998	OKE				34.26		1,000	1,000		
1999	OKE	34.26	1.24	3.62%	24.84	-23.88%	761	1,160		
2000	OKE	24.84	1.24	4.99%	48.12	98.71%	1,513	1,347	1.46	16.48
2001	OKE	24.06	0.62	2.58%	17.84	-23.28%	1,161	1,563	0.85	10.49
2002	OKE	17.84	0.62	3.48%	19.20	11.10%	1,289	1,813	1.39	13.81
2003	OKE	19.20	0.69	3.59%	22.08	18.59%	1,529	2,104	1.22	18.10
2004	OKE	22.08	0.88	3.99%	28.42	32.70%	2,029	2,442	2.30	12.36
2005	OKE	28.42	1.09	3.84%	26.63	-2.46%	1,979	2,833	2.34	11.38
2006	OKE	26.63	1.22	4.58%	43.12	66.50%	3,295	3,288	1.98	21.78
2007	OKE	43.12	1.40	3.25%	44.77	7.07%	3,529	3,815	2.83	15.82
2008	OKE	44.77	1.56	3.48%	29.12	-31.47%	2,418	4,427	2.97	9.80
2009	OKE	29.12	1.66	5.70%	44.57	58.76%	3,839	5,137	2.80	15.92
2010	OKE	44.57	1.82	4.08%	55.47	28.54%	4,934	5,961	3.09	17.95
2011	OKE	55.47	2.16	3.89%	86.69	60.18%	7,904	6,917	3.34	25.96
2012	OKE	43.35	1.27	2.93%	42.75	1.56%	8,027	8,027	1.76	24.29

		DIA	SPY	XLU	2012	Cumul	Fiscal yr end
	Cumulative	10.68%	8.69%	0.66%	127.48%	5 yr	31-Dec
	Cumulative	94.13%	95.71%	158.75%	522.52%	10 yr	
	Cumulative	90.91%	46.69%	89.63%	702.68%	14 yr	

Spreadsheet 6.27 American Electric Power

Year Ending 31-Dec	XLU Utilities-Electricity Sym	Begin Price	Div	Div Pct	End Price	Gain Loss	Value	Yearly Ave Tot Ret 7.15%	Year End EPS	P/E
1999	AEP						1,000	1,000		
2000	AEP	32.13	2.40	7.47%	46.50	52.19%	1,522	1,072		
2001	AEP	46.50	2.40	5.16%	43.53	-1.23%	1,503	1,148	2.98	15.60
2002	AEP	43.53	2.40	5.51%	27.33	-31.70%	1,027	1,230	1.46	29.82
2003	AEP	27.33	1.65	6.04%	30.51	17.67%	1,208	1,318	1.36	20.10
2004	AEP	30.51	1.40	4.59%	34.34	17.14%	1,415	1,412	2.84	10.74
2005	AEP	34.34	1.42	4.14%	37.09	12.14%	1,587	1,513	2.63	13.06
2006	AEP	37.09	1.50	4.04%	42.58	18.85%	1,886	1,622	2.50	14.84
2007	AEP	42.58	1.58	3.71%	46.56	13.06%	2,133	1,738	2.86	14.89
2008	AEP	46.56	1.64	3.52%	33.28	-25.00%	1,599	1,862	3.39	13.73
2009	AEP	33.28	1.64	4.93%	34.79	9.47%	1,751	1,995	2.97	11.21
2010	AEP	34.79	1.71	4.92%	35.98	8.34%	1,897	2,138	2.53	13.75
2011	AEP	35.98	1.85	5.14%	41.31	19.96%	2,275	2,290	4.02	8.95
2012	AEP	41.31	1.88	4.55%	42.68	7.87%	2,454	2,454	4.00	10.33
				DIA	SPY	XLU	2012	Cumul	Fiscal yr end	
			Cumulative	10.68%	8.69%	0.66%	15.09%	5 yr	31-Dec	
			Cumulative	94.13%	95.71%	158.75%	139.04%	10 yr		
			Cumulative	90.91%	46.69%	89.63%		14 yr		

Spreadsheet 6.28 Westar Energy

Year Ending 31-Dec	XLU Utilities-Electricity Sym	Begin Price	Div	Div Pct	End Price	Gain Loss	Value	Yearly Ave Tot Ret 4.71%	Year End EPS	P/E
1998	WR				33.25		1,000	1,000		
1999	WR	33.25	2.14	6.44%	16.94	-42.62%	574	1,047		
2000	WR	16.94	1.44	8.47%	24.81	54.93%	889	1,096	2.03	8.34
2001	WR	24.81	1.20	4.84%	17.20	-25.84%	659	1,148	0.81	30.63
2002	WR	17.20	1.20	6.98%	9.90	-35.47%	426	1,202	1.22	14.10
2003	WR	9.90	0.76	7.68%	20.25	112.22%	903	1,259	2.20	4.50
2004	WR	20.25	0.80	3.95%	22.87	16.89%	1,056	1,318	1.19	17.02
2005	WR	22.87	0.92	4.02%	21.50	-1.97%	1,035	1,380	1.53	14.95
2006	WR	21.50	1.00	4.65%	25.96	25.40%	1,298	1,445	1.87	11.50
2007	WR	25.96	1.08	4.16%	25.94	4.08%	1,351	1,514	1.83	14.19
2008	WR	25.94	1.16	4.47%	20.51	-16.46%	1,128	1,585	1.69	15.35
2009	WR	20.51	1.20	5.85%	21.72	11.75%	1,261	1,660	1.28	16.02
2010	WR	21.72	1.24	5.71%	25.16	21.55%	1,532	1,738	1.80	12.07
2011	WR	25.16	1.28	5.09%	28.78	19.48%	1,831	1,820	1.96	12.84
2012	WR	28.78	1.32	4.59%	28.62	4.03%	1,905	1,905		
				DIA	SPY	XLU	2012	Cumul	Fiscal yr end	
			Cumulative	10.68%	8.69%	0.66%	41.03%	5 yr	31-Dec	
			Cumulative	94.13%	95.71%	158.75%	347.63%	10 yr		
			Cumulative	90.91%	46.69%	89.63%	90.47%	14 yr		

CHAPTER SEVEN
MASTER LIMITED PARTNERSHIPS (MLPs)

Yes, I've decided that this complex subject deserves a chapter all its own. Warning: this chapter will in all probability be the most difficult in this book to understand if you haven't already studied MLPs. Much has been written about MLPs. It seems that most every investment advisor believes they understand them. They just understand them differently than the next advisor.

MLPs were created by the 1986 Tax Reform Act. This was done to encourage investment in U.S. natural resources and pipelines. MLPs avoid federal tax at the corporate level. Federal taxes are passed through to the unit holders. A share in an MLP is referred to as a 'Unit', not a share of stock. What is a dividend to a stock is a 'distribution' to an MLP. A distribution can be a return of capital and/or a capital gain.

Master Limited Partnerships are primarily engaged in exploring, marketing, mining, processing, producing, refining, storing or transporting any mineral or natural resource. MLPs are divided into three types:

1) Upstream MLPs:
   Upstream MLPs are engaged primarily in the production of oil and natural gas.

2) Midstream MLPs:
   Midstream MLPs are engaged in the gathering, processing, storing and transporting of oil, natural gas and refined petroleum products such as propane gas. These are by far the most numerous. They are also commonly referred to as 'Pipeline Companies'.

3) Downstream MLPs:
   These would be the oil refineries.

Taxable Accounts:

In taxable accounts, distributions are considered return of capital, which means you are not taxed right away but likely would mean a big taxable capital gain when the units are sold. Each distribution you receive will lower your basis (original investment) in the 'units'. If you were to hold your units for many years without selling, your basis could go to zero. Your basis can not go below zero. Once you have recovered all of your original investment, you would have to start paying taxes each year on all of your distribution. In most cases, this would not happen until you have owned the same MLP for eight to ten years. These distributions would be taxed as a capital gain under current tax law.

If you have a large investment in a taxable account, be sure to look at your IRS form K-1 when you receive it, to see if you owe any ***state income tax in any of the states that your MLP does business***. Please see your tax advisor if this fits your situation.

There is only one ETF that I know of that invests primarily in MLPs. This is the Alerian MLP Exchange Traded Fund (ETF) ticker (AMLP). The fund expense is 0.85%. According to their website investors will receive a Form 1099 at the end of each tax year. There will not be a K-1 or any state tax filings to be concerned about. However the returns on Alerian, even though they run full page ads in Barron's, have not been as good as the ETNs discussed below.

Exchange Traded Notes

'Exchange Traded Notes' (ETNs) are not the same as 'Exchange Traded Funds' (ETFs). There is somewhat of a difference that deserves an explanation. Here are some basic fundamental differences between the two. ETFs are a fund of actual stocks. ETNs have different characteristics.

1) **ETNs do not actually hold any securities:**

Instead, an issuing bank is obligated to pay investors an amount reflected by the performance of the index it tracks minus any fees. ETFs are seen as investment companies.

2) The basic structure is different:
   a) ETNs are regulated under the 'Securities Act of 1933'.
   b) ETFs come under the regulation of the 'Investment Company Act of 1940'.

These two acts probably seem like a small difference, but this is the basis of the difference between the two, including taxation.

3) Debt or Equity:
   a) ETNs are considered debt instruments, which are usually unsecured debt by the issuing party. This means that in the unlikely event the issuing firm (probably JP Morgan or UBS) were to go bankrupt; investors would have to get in line with other creditors. Since they are technically debt they must have a maturity date like a bond, about thirty years after the issue date. Then, it is supposed to be paid out like a bond at maturity. But since ETNs are a new concept, who knows what will happen before we have to deal with this.
   b) ETFs on the other hand, are equity because they must purchase most of the MLPs units in the index. If the issuer were to go bankrupt your ETF issuer such as I-Shares or PowerShares, the investor's capital is safe.

4) Elimination of Tracking Error
   a) Since ETNs do not go out and buy the actual securities in the index. It's easier to replicate the index with futures and options.
   b) ETFs do have to purchase securities in the index that closely replicate the desired index. Some securities in an index might not be very liquid and this can cause minor tracking problems in the smaller market capitalization MLPs.

Furthermore, if ETFs were to own futures then investors would receive a K-1 at tax time. ETNs, being the debt instruments that they are, do not face this problem. My theory is: ETNs were created, at least in part, in order to eliminate the notorious K-1 and eliminate the possibly of investors having to pay state taxes to numerous states just because the pipelines go through these states. Maybe, just maybe the lobbyists did a good turn for investors in this case.

A taxable account investor who wants to avoid the K-1s and the various states taxes could avoid this by investing in the following 'Exchange Traded Notes (ETNs):

J.P. Morgan-Alerian MLP Index Exchange Traded Note (AMJ)
This fund has by far the largest amount of net assets ($5 Billion)
The inception date for this fund was April 1, 2009.

UBS E-TRACS Alerian MLP Infrastructure ETN (MLPI)
This fund has net assets of about $395 million.
The inception date for this fund was March 31, 2010.

UBS E-TRACS Alerian Natural Gas MLP Index ETN (MLPG)
This fund has net assets of only $15 million.
The inception date for this fund was July 12, 2010

Tax Deferred Accounts

We really can't discuss MLPs without looking at the tax deferred account implications, even for a Roth IRA. First, you are allowed to buy MLP unit shares in your tax advantaged account even though some advisers advise against it. This is probably because it means a little extra work on their part. Next, tax exempt institutions and retirement accounts must pay tax on their "Unrelated Business Taxable Income "(UBTI). But many MLPs do not have any 'UBTI' or even have negative UBTI. The good news is that, if the MLP does have 'UBTI' each tax advantaged account currently has a $1,000 exemption. This is not a limit on your distribution; it's just on the UBTI portion of your distribution. You can find more detailed and up to date information on the 'National Association of Publicly Traded Partnerships' website at www.naptp.org. To be safe, under current tax law you should not owe any additional tax from your tax advantaged account as long as your *unrelated business taxable income'* (UBTI) distributions shown on your K-1 are under $1,000 each year in *each account*. As always check with your tax advisor for the latest information.

If all else fails and you go over the $1,000 limit, you will not pay the tax directly on your tax return. It will be your retirement account custodian's responsibility to file the form (990) and pay the tax owed out of the account's funds.

As we go to press here in early 2013 the Alerian MLP Index is up far more than the S&P 500 Index in the last fifteen years. And let's not forget the much higher distributions that have been paid by MLPs. Please look at the total returns of the various MLPs at the end of this chapter. The average yield for an MLP is around 6% whereas the S&P 500 yield is in the 2% range.

In conclusion, if you are a taxable account investor, MLPs are a highly recommended investment that is tailor made for you. If you are a high net worth investor then you might want to use some ETNs to avoid the K-1s and especially the multiple states that you could have to pay taxes to.

Spreadsheet 7.1 MLPs Magellan Midstream Partners

Year Ending 31-Dec	Sym	Begin Price	Div	Div Pct	End Price	Gain Loss	Value	Yearly Ave Tot Ret 19.77%	EPS	Year End P/E
2001	MMP				41.80		1,000	1,000	0.93	
2002	MMP	41.80	1.36	3.24%	32.45	-19.12%	809	1,198	1.84	22.72
2003	MMP	32.45	1.59	4.88%	50.00	58.97%	1,286	1,434	1.66	19.55
2004	MMP	50.00	1.76	3.52%	58.67	20.86%	1,554	1,718	1.72	29.07
2005	MMP	29.34	2.06	7.03%	32.23	16.90%	1,816	2,058	2.03	14.45
2006	MMP	32.23	2.34	7.24%	38.60	27.01%	2,307	2,464	2.27	14.20
2007	MMP	38.60	2.55	6.60%	43.36	18.93%	2,744	2,952	2.69	14.35
2008	MMP	43.36	2.77	6.38%	30.21	-23.94%	2,087	3,535	2.21	19.62
2009	MMP	30.21	2.84	9.40%	43.33	52.83%	3,189	4,234	2.22	13.61
2010	MMP	43.33	2.91	6.71%	56.50	37.10%	4,373	5,071	2.85	15.20
2011	MMP	56.50	3.10	5.48%	68.88	27.39%	5,570	6,074	3.66	15.44
2012	MMP	34.44	1.78	5.18%	43.19	30.59%	7,274	7,274		
				DIA	SPY	XLE	2012	Cumul	Fiscal yr end	
			Cumulative	10.68%	8.69%	-2.15%	165.11%	5 yr	31-Dec	
			Cumulative	94.13%	95.71%	270.76%	799.39%	10 yr		
			Cumulative	90.91%	46.69%	283.04%		14 yr		

Spreadsheet 7.2 MLPs Energy Transfer Partners

Year Ending 31-Dec	Sym	Begin Price	Div	Div Pct	End Price	Gain Loss	Value	Yearly Ave Tot Ret 19.59%	EPS	Year End P/E
1998	ETP				20.32		1,000	1,000		
1999	ETP	20.32	2.19	10.78%	18.38	1.23%	1,012	1,196		
2000	ETP	18.38	2.26	12.32%	22.50	34.73%	1,364	1,430	(0.19)	
2001	ETP	22.50	2.43	10.78%	29.65	42.56%	1,944	1,710	0.71	31.69
2002	ETP	29.65	2.55	8.60%	28.20	3.71%	2,016	2,045	0.13	228.08
2003	ETP	28.20	2.56	9.09%	41.24	55.33%	3,132	2,446	3.00	9.40
2004	ETP	41.24	2.93	7.09%	59.20	50.64%	4,718	2,925	1.61	25.61
2005	ETP	29.60	1.89	6.38%	34.24	22.05%	5,759	3,498	1.09	27.16
2006	ETP	34.24	2.56	7.47%	54.10	65.47%	9,529	4,183	3.15	10.87
2007	ETP	54.10	4.31	7.97%	53.88	7.56%	10,250	5,003	3.37	16.05
2008	ETP	53.88	3.81	7.06%	34.01	-29.81%	7,194	5,983	3.83	14.07
2009	ETP	34.01	3.58	10.51%	44.97	42.74%	10,269	7,155	2.54	13.39
2010	ETP	44.97	3.58	7.95%	51.82	23.18%	12,649	8,556	1.52	29.59
2011	ETP	51.82	3.58	6.90%	45.85	-4.62%	12,065	10,233	2.60	19.93
2012	ETP	45.85	3.58	7.80%	42.93	1.43%	12,237	12,237		
				DIA	SPY	XLE	2012	Cumul	Fiscal yr end	
			Cumulative	10.68%	8.69%	-2.15%	19.38%	5 yr	31-Dec	
			Cumulative	94.13%	95.71%	270.76%	506.85%	10 yr	31-Aug	
			Cumulative	90.91%	46.69%	283.04%	1123.71%	14 yr		

Spreadsheet 7.3 MLPs Kinder Morgan Energy Partners

Year Ending 31-Dec	Sym	Begin Price	Div	Div Pct	End Price	Gain Loss	Value	Yearly Ave Tot Ret	Year End EPS	Year End P/E
1998	KMP				36.25		1,000	17.54%		
1999	KMP	36.25	1.39	3.83%	41.44	18.14%	1,181	1,175	1.31	27.67
2000	KMP	41.44	1.60	3.86%	56.31	39.74%	1,651	1,382	1.34	30.93
2001	KMP	28.16	1.31	4.66%	37.82	38.99%	2,295	1,624	1.56	18.05
2002	KMP	37.82	2.36	6.24%	35.00	-1.22%	2,267	1,909	1.96	19.30
2003	KMP	35.00	2.58	7.36%	49.27	48.13%	3,358	2,244	1.98	17.68
2004	KMP	49.27	2.81	5.70%	44.33	-4.32%	3,213	2,637	2.22	22.19
2005	KMP	44.33	3.07	6.93%	47.82	14.80%	3,688	3,100	1.58	28.06
2006	KMP	47.82	3.23	6.75%	47.90	6.92%	3,943	3,643	2.12	22.56
2007	KMP	47.90	3.39	7.08%	53.99	19.79%	4,724	4,283	0.55	87.09
2008	KMP	53.99	3.89	7.21%	45.75	-8.06%	4,343	5,034	1.94	27.83
2009	KMP	45.75	4.20	9.18%	60.98	42.47%	6,188	5,917	4.20	10.89
2010	KMP	60.98	4.32	7.08%	70.26	22.30%	7,568	6,955	2.50	24.39
2011	KMP	70.26	4.58	6.52%	84.95	27.43%	9,643	8,175	3.50	20.07
2012	KMP	84.95	4.85	5.71%	79.79	-0.36%	9,608	9,608		
				DIA	SPY	XLE	2012	Cumul	Fiscal yr end	
			Cumulative	10.68%	8.69%	-2.15%	103.40%	5 yr	31-Dec	
			Cumulative	94.13%	95.71%	270.76%	323.86%	10 yr		
			Cumulative	90.91%	46.69%	283.04%	860.81%	14 yr		

Spreadsheet 7.4 MLPs Buckeye Partners

Year Ending 31-Dec	Sym	Begin Price	Div	Div Pct	End Price	Gain Loss	Value	Yearly Ave Tot Ret	Year End EPS	Year End P/E
1998					26.21		1,000	11.41%		
1999	BPL	26.21	2.18	8.30%	25.43	5.32%	1,053	1,114	2.60	10.08
2000	BPL	25.43	2.40	9.44%	28.88	23.00%	1,296	1,241	2.34	10.87
2001	BPL	28.88	2.45	8.48%	37.48	38.26%	1,791	1,383	2.53	11.42
2002	BPL	37.48	2.50	6.67%	38.40	9.12%	1,955	1,541	2.62	14.31
2003	BPL	38.40	2.54	6.61%	45.35	24.71%	2,438	1,717	1.04	36.92
2004	BPL	45.35	2.64	5.82%	42.32	-0.87%	2,416	1,913	2.75	16.49
2005	BPL	42.32	2.83	6.68%	42.22	6.44%	2,572	2,131	2.69	15.73
2006	BPL	42.22	3.03	7.16%	46.48	17.25%	3,016	2,374	2.63	16.05
2007	BPL	46.48	3.23	6.94%	49.41	13.24%	3,415	2,645	2.91	15.97
2008	BPL	49.41	3.43	6.93%	32.25	-27.80%	2,466	2,947	1.33	37.15
2009	BPL	32.25	3.63	11.24%	54.45	80.08%	4,440	3,284	2.49	12.95
2010	BPL	54.45	3.83	7.02%	66.83	29.76%	5,762	3,658	1.65	33.00
2011	BPL	66.83	4.03	6.02%	63.98	1.76%	5,863	4,076	1.20	55.69
2012	BPL	63.98	4.14	6.47%	45.41	-22.56%	4,541	4,541		
				DIA	SPY	XLE	2012	Cumul	Fiscal yr end	
			Cumulative	10.68%	8.69%	-2.15%	32.95%	5 yr	31-Dec	
			Cumulative	94.13%	95.71%	270.76%	132.30%	10 yr		
			Cumulative	90.91%	46.69%	283.04%	354.07%	14 yr		

Spreadsheet 7.5 MLPs NuStar Energy LP

Year Ending 31-Dec	Sym	Begin Price	Div	Div Pct	End Price	Gain Loss	Value	Yearly Ave Tot Ret 8.31%	Year End EPS	P/E
2001	N S				37.82		1,000	1,000		
2002	N S	37.82	2.65	7.01%	39.70	11.98%	1,120	1,083	2.72	13.90
2003	N S	39.70	2.90	7.30%	49.77	32.67%	1,486	1,173	3.02	13.15
2004	N S	49.77	3.15	6.33%	59.43	25.74%	1,868	1,271	3.15	15.80
2005	N S	59.43	3.31	5.57%	51.76	-7.34%	1,731	1,376	2.77	21.45
2006	N S	51.76	3.54	6.84%	55.77	14.59%	1,983	1,491	2.84	18.23
2007	N S	55.77	3.77	6.75%	53.30	2.32%	2,029	1,615	2.73	20.43
2008	N S	53.30	4.01	7.53%	41.06	-15.44%	1,716	1,749	4.22	12.63
2009	N S	41.06	4.24	10.32%	56.09	46.93%	2,522	1,894	3.47	11.83
2010	N S	56.09	4.27	7.61%	69.48	31.49%	3,315	2,052	3.19	17.58
2011	N S	69.48	4.34	6.25%	56.66	-12.20%	2,911	2,222	2.78	24.99
2012	N S	56.66	4.38	7.73%	42.48	-17.30%	2,407	2,407		
				DIA	SPY	XLE	2012	Cumul	Fiscal yr end	
			Cumulative	10.68%	8.69%	-2.15%	18.62%	5 yr	31-Dec	
			Cumulative	94.13%	95.71%	270.76%	114.98%	10 yr		
			Cumulative	90.91%	46.69%	283.04%		14 yr		

Spreadsheet 7.6 MLPs AmeriGas Partners

Year Ending 31-Dec	Sym	Begin Price	Div	Div Pct	End Price	Gain Loss	Value	Yearly Ave Tot Ret 13.91%	Year End EPS	P/E
1998	A P U				19.97		1,000	1,000		
1999	A P U	19.97	2.20	11.02%	14.60	-15.87%	841	1,139		
2000	A P U	14.60	2.20	15.07%	16.62	28.90%	1,084	1,298		
2001	A P U	16.62	2.20	13.24%	22.37	47.83%	1,603	1,478		
2002	A P U	22.37	2.20	9.83%	23.85	16.45%	1,867	1,684		
2003	A P U	23.85	2.20	9.22%	28.01	26.67%	2,365	1,918	1.42	16.80
2004	A P U	28.01	2.20	7.85%	29.60	13.53%	2,685	2,185	1.71	16.38
2005	A P U	29.60	2.23	7.53%	28.27	3.04%	2,766	2,488	1.10	26.91
2006	A P U	28.27	2.30	8.14%	32.53	23.20%	3,408	2,835	1.59	17.78
2007	A P U	32.53	2.66	8.18%	36.04	18.97%	4,055	3,229	3.26	9.98
2008	A P U	36.04	2.53	7.02%	28.13	-14.93%	3,449	3,678	2.73	13.20
2009	A P U	28.13	2.82	10.02%	39.33	49.84%	5,169	4,190	3.59	7.84
2010	A P U	39.33	2.79	7.08%	48.81	31.18%	6,780	4,772	2.80	14.05
2011	A P U	48.81	2.93	5.99%	45.91	0.05%	6,784	5,436	2.30	21.22
2012	A P U	45.91	3.16	6.89%	38.74	-8.73%	6,192	6,192		
				DIA	SPY	XLE	2012	Cumul	Fiscal yr end	
			Cumulative	10.68%	8.69%	-2.15%	52.71%	5 yr	30-Sep	
			Cumulative	94.13%	95.71%	270.76%	231.66%	10 yr		
			Cumulative	90.91%	46.69%	283.04%	519.17%	14 yr		

CHAPTER EIGHT
FIXED INCOME

Corporate Bonds

As we go to press, U.S. Government Treasuries are paying a little more than 3% and that's for the thirty year variety. Short term treasuries of one year or less are paying less than 1%. When it comes to investing in bonds, the first thing you should understand is *how* they come to be rated AAA (best) or BBB+ (the lowest investment grade) all the way down to D (in default). The rating system on corporate bonds is, in my not so humble opinion, very flawed. It goes like this: A corporation wants to issue some bonds. They can go to one or more of the major rating agencies for a rating. The major rating agencies are Standard and Poor, Moody's and Fitch. The rating agencies get paid by the *issuer of the bonds*. Talk about conflict of interest, this is a blatant example of just that. So the issuer can shop around for the best, not necessarily the most accurate ratings. Ratings *should be* independent and unbiased which obviously they are not. Remember the meltdown of 2008, some of the securitized debt was rated AAA, when it should have been rated CCC at best. Thanks to heavy lobbying by the financial services industry the rules basically still haven't changed even in early 2013.

Keep in mind that the issuer can choose not to be rated. This most always means the issuing company knows they will not get a satisfactory (to them) rating, and they are not willing to pay for a low rating. When a bond issue isn't rated by a major agency you should see a 'NR' under the rating heading.

Corporate bonds, even AAA rated are always going to pay a small premium interest rate to the government issues. Many of the AAA rated bonds are currently paying less than 3.5% on their thirty year maturity bonds. The question becomes how much risk are you willing to take? As with any investing you usually must be willing to take greater risk to get a greater reward. But even investment grade (BBB+ and above) corporate bonds are only paying about 6% on the thirty year bonds. With interest rates at record lows but slowly rising here in early 2013 it's strongly recommended that you stay away from any long term treasuries or long term corporate bonds because, once interest rates start heading up you will suffer a capital loss.

When you are retired and hopefully the interest rates go up a little you should consider '*laddering your bonds*'. Laddering is a good and safe way to draw down your savings and give you a dependable income. To do this you simply buy a group of bonds that mature in successive years in the future time frame you want to cover. It will also keep you from locking in low interest rates on your entire bond portfolio.

Preferred Stocks

Preferred stocks are the Rodney Dangerfield's of the investment world. They just don't get any respect. I recently went to a 'Money Show' in Orlando, Florida and of all the presentations there I could not find even one on any preferred stock.

In today's investing environment, cumulative preferred stocks offer a very good way to manage your short term cash needs while we wait for the inevitable rise in interest rates. Preferred stocks are also known as hybrids because they are stocks and because, they are equity in the company. They are also bond like because; they eventually mature in thirty to forty years in some cases. In addition, like bonds, preferred stocks can be redeemed early (after the initial redemption date) *at the option* of the issuer. Keep in mind, that in today's low interest rate environment some issuers will call a preferred issue, and turn right around and issue another preferred stock to replace it with a lower dividend rate.

When it comes to the preferred stock dividend, these dividends must be paid *before* or at the same time the common stock dividend is paid. Dividends are most always paid quarterly just like common stocks. A good way to evaluate the risk of owning a preferred stock, or a bond, is to look at the common stock dividend history if the company pays one. Obviously, if the company is profitable and paying a nice common stock dividend the preferred share dividends and the bond interest payments should be much safer. The dividends on most all preferred stocks are fixed just like bond interest payments. However, the one major difference between a bond and a preferred stock is: If the preferred stock does not make its dividend payment on time it *does not* go into default the way a bond would. Keep in mind that in the event of bankruptcy or liquidation bondholders are in line ahead of any stockholders (including preferred). Preferred stockholders are usually only in line ahead of the common stockholders.

Most preferred stock shares are issued at $25.00 per share, and this is most always the price of redemption (at the option of the issuer), or the price paid at maturity when it must be paid in full (like a bond). When you are considering a purchase in the secondary market, and for example an issue is selling for $25.50 per share, this is a 2% premium to what you will be paid at redemption, and just like a bond you should calculate the yield to worst (YTW). This would be the earliest date the preferred could be redeemed by the issuer.

One disadvantage about preferred stocks is that it is difficult to get diversification. Most of the issuers come from REITs, banks and utilities. For example, if the above preferred stock has two years before it can be redeemed a 6% stated rate would only net you 5% annually if redeemed at the earliest redeemed date by the issuer. Most of all you should be very careful if the issue is selling at a premium, and it is past the date it can be redeemed. You could lose whatever premium you paid for the preferred share of stock if it were to be called at par right away. Let's keep in mind during the slow economic recovery we are currently experiencing the Federal Reserve Board (who sets interest rate policy in the U.S.) has committed to keep short term interest rates at just above 0.00% until sometime in 2015. But, just like with long term bonds, once the interest rates start to raise it will in all probability be a good time to sell your preferred stocks to prevent a capital loss, unless they are near their maturity date, and just hold cash until money market rates and / or bond rates go up.

Preferred stock prices can be inefficient and that can work in your favor. Theoretically, on the date when any stock (common or preferred) goes ex-dividend the price drops by the dividend amount, because if you were to buy the stock on or after that date you are not entitled to the next dividend payment. This (dropping of the price) is not always true with preferred stocks. Most preferred stocks go ex-dividend about two weeks before the dividend is paid. On average this is a shorter time frame than common stocks. So, if you were to buy a preferred issue one day before it goes ex-dividend and sell it one year later after it goes ex-dividend, you could collect five dividend payments for a holding period of about 370 days. The reason for this inefficiency is twofold. One, preferred stocks are not nearly as closely followed as common stocks. The other reason is the market tends to think of preferred stocks as bond like, which they are. If the preferred issue were to be called in the middle of the quarter, you would be paid your prorated dividend. If you are close to or past the date at which the issue can be redeemed it is likely the preferred issue will be trading very close to par (usually $25).

There Are Two Types of Preferred Stock:

Cumulative Preferred Stock

Cumulative preferred means that if the dividend is suspended, the dividend that is owed to you accumulates and that *no common stock dividend can be paid* until all of the dividends in arrears on the preferred shares are paid up to date. The difference between the preferred stock and a bond is that a bond is considered debt and preferred stock is considered equity. If the interest is not paid on a bond it is in default and the issuer can be forced into bankruptcy. In today's investing environment (Early 2013) I prefer the cumulative preferred stocks to bonds for the short to medium term (0-4 years) because of the higher rates of return for very little additional risk. These cumulative preferred stocks have the least risk.

Non-Cumulative Preferred Stock

Non Cumulative means that if the dividend is suspended, the dividend *does not accumulate* even though *no common stock dividend* can be paid until the preferred stock dividends are resumed, but the missed dividend payments *are not made up*. The good news is that this type of preferred share will usually carry a slightly higher dividend.

Preferred Stock Information

The big disadvantage with any preferred stocks is the information available is both hard to find and difficult to interpret, but with a little help you can learn to navigate it. Preferred stocks are listed in Barron's each week but without the ticker symbols the issues are hard to identify. In addition they usually don't offer any commentary. Some of the websites that give great information on common stocks often give little or no information on preferred stocks.

I have access to Morningstar and I have found this to be a good information source for preferred stocks. By far the best *free* website I have found for preferred stock information is 'www.preferredstockchannel.com'. You can just enter the common stock symbol and it will list the preferred shares that are currently trading with the same company. It also has all the fundamentals on both the common and preferred issue on the same page for your evaluation. It also lists preferred stocks by industry.

Trading Symbols

The trading symbols of common stocks are standard throughout the financial industry. However the preferred issues are a mixed bag to say the least. Below is an example of how one of my issues is listed with various entities.

One of my former holdings is the banking stock BB&T, common stock symbol (BBT). The preferred (Preferred B) issue that I owned separately is listed as follows:

Yahoo	BBT-PB
MSN Money	BBT-B
Morningstar	BBTPRB
E*Trade	BBT.PR.B

As you can see the financial services industry hasn't yet come up with a standard trading symbol way of listing preferred stocks.

Preferred Stock Fundamentals:

Let's keep in mind the main features of preferred stocks in the United States:

- Preference over common stock in receiving dividends.
- Preference over common stock in the event of asset liquidation.
- If a company has many different preferred issues then there is most likely a pecking order of the different issues in case of liquidation.
- In some cases it is convertible to common stock.
- It is callable (after the redemption date) at the option of the issuer.
- Non Voting in most cases.

CHAPTER NINE
A LITTLE SPECULATION

When it comes to speculation please don't bet money that you can't afford to lose. It's recommended that you don't go over 10% of your portfolio in this high risk category. This is definitely higher risk than we have discussed previously. It is really about picking a bottom in the stock or the market. Please keep in mind that this is not an exact science. Several clichés come to mind when trying to do this:

- Be fearful when the market is greedy and be greedy when the market is fearful.
- The best time to buy stocks is when there is blood in the streets.
- Don't try to catch a falling knife.

When we are trying to find a bottom it is a good time to apply a little bit of technical analysis. Whether it's a stock or an ETF don't buy when the chart line is heading straight down. (That's the falling knife). At least wait until the chart line has moved sideways for a few days. This is definitely the time when the market is usually very *fearful* and the time **we want to be greedy.**

Success with Ford

OK, now please bear with me while I brag just a little. As I stated previously I worked for Chrysler for over forty-four years. I am sure you know the auto industry has been very cyclical over the last sixty years, and in the fall of 2008 we had the Big Three Automaker CEOs going to Washington DC asking for a government bailout. I'm not going to express any political view here because it does not and should not matter to investors. The subject here is investing. What matters *"**to us investors is how we can make money off of what is likely to happen**"*.

Chrysler and General Motors went in to what was referred to as a controlled bankruptcy. General Motors became a penny stock. Chrysler had been previously taken private in 2007, a year and a half before the really bad news. Contrary to popular belief Ford did not take any bailout money from the federal government. Ford stock was trading at over $37.00 per share on April 12, 1999. On April 28, 2008 the stock had dropped to a little over $8.00 per share. By November 17, 2008 the common stock was trading in the $1.40 per share range, a 25 year low. My feeling at that time based on publicly available factual information was as follows:

- The Ford family still owned about 40% of the voting shares of stock and they were not selling.
- The Ford family was sticking together and sticking by the company with their family name on it.
- Contrary to the popular belief on Wall Street, Ford had a better working relationship with the Union (UAW) than either General Motors or Chrysler and this was very important.
- By working in the industry I felt there was almost no chance of a strike over the sacrifices from the workers that were coming which would have made the recovery much more difficult if not impossible.
- I knew the UAW and Ford would work together with both of their futures hanging in the balance. William Clay Ford Jr. the great-grandson of the founder Henry Ford was humble enough to step down as CEO and hire Alan Mulally, formally from Boeing as CEO. Mr. Mulally is a top flight manager from a manufacturing company that has experience working with unions in a cyclical industry. Even though that's not the company I was working for (but the same industry) I could see that Ford had much better leadership than the other domestic auto companies, and was in a much position to come out of the deep recession we were in.

The facts were soon to prove me correct. Soon after my last purchase of Ford in January 2009, Rick Wagoner the General Motors CEO was asked to step down by President Obama in March 2009. My employer, Chrysler, had gone through a lot of recent turmoil. First we had recently been split off from DaimlerChrysler in 2007 only about nine years after the infamous *'merger of (un) equals'* in 1998. Chrysler was sold to Cerberus and soon after Bob Nardelli was installed as CEO. Let's just say, I knew Bob Nardelli was no 'Lee Iacocca' the great (in my opinion) Chrysler CEO from 1978-1992.

The way it looked to me, at that time, the market was throwing out the baby with the bath water. One or even two domestic automotive companies might go out of business but I felt very strongly that Ford would be left standing. Ford could even benefit if one of the other domestic companies went out of business, which did not happen.

Ford CEO Alan Mulally did go to Washington, DC on a private jet with the other automotive industry CEOs, but he **did not** ask the Federal Government for a bailout, even though Ford's stock was still trading at less than $2.50 per share. This fact made me feel that Ford was deeply oversold. I felt that all of the clichés mentioned earlier in this chapter were in place and that it was time for me to act. It was clear to me that even though its CEO was at that time fairly new to the company, Ford was positioned for a strong comeback. I knew from past business cycles that when you wait for Wall Street to recommend domestic automotive stocks then much of the money has already been made and it's almost time to sell. So between November 2008 and February 2009 I bought Ford (F) common stock in two different purchases, some at $2.49 per share and some at $2.42 per share. By the time my investment in Ford had more than tripled to about $8.00 per share, Jim Cramer on CNBCs 'Mad Money' was bragging about his recommending Ford at $5.00 per share, and he was one of the first on Wall Street to do so.

I sold my first batch in October 2009 at $7.06 per share. With what I had left I was now playing with "the house's money". Did I sell too soon? Yes, we all have 100% hindsight but I still had a lot of shares left. In a situation like this: after a big run up of a deep cyclical stock you should take some money off the table. One negative announcement could send the stock down again. When it almost doubled again at $13.00 in March 2010 I sold another batch as it was at a six year high. I still had more shares left that I sold at $16.70 in December 2010. Ford common stock topped out in January 2011 at $18.97 per share. Then when it dropped to $14.00 per share in March 2011 I sold the last of my shares because it seemed to be heading back down. This was more than a 26% drop from the recent high. Ford went on to trade at less than $9.00 per share in the Summer of 2012.

As we go to press there is a feel good attitude about Ford right now as it is trading in the $13.00-$14.00 per share range. They have just announced a doubling of the dividend to $0.40 annually. Wall Street is beginning to like the stock again. Are they a buy and hold forever stock? Go back and look at the first few words in the cliché at the beginning of this chapter. It would be too risky to buy Ford again before we are in the middle of the *next* recession. If you had owned Ford continuously since 1971 you would have a total return of a little over 8% per year. If you had owned Ford common stock since 1998 your total return would have been negative. This is way under the long term market average total return of around 10% per year, and it has been on a roller coaster ride that you shouldn't want to take. This stock is not a long term hold.

A look at what I believe to be a political bias is that: Wall Street just hates labor unions and always wants to believe their industries are doomed to failure. This has turned out to be wishful thinking in at least some instances and a missed opportunity for the people who took their advice. I'm sure this is not always the case, but keep in mind that it could be when making your investment decisions, especially if you want to invest in the auto industry or other deep cyclical stocks from time to time. Perception is not always the reality. Even the professionals on Wall Street sometimes get it all wrong. After reading this chapter you can understand that they can let their biases get in the way of stock evaluation. You can use this example to help you in evaluating whatever industry you might work in or have professional knowledge of. Public perception is not always reality and you can profit from it. See Spreadsheet 9.1.

Goodyear Tire and Rubber (GT)

Goodyear Tire has been in business since 1898. But the best thing I can say about the last forty years is *that it has survived*. It's a deep cyclical auto parts industry stock. Take a look at the charts on this stock. If you can buy in at the right time you can do well in the short term. However, it is a very risky stock, much more so than Ford. If you had bought Goodyear in 1970 and held it until the end of 2012 your total return would have been about 3.1% per year. Study this stock very carefully before you invest. If you decide to buy this stock you need a disciplined exit plan. See Spreadsheet 9.2.

The Boeing Company (BA)

My records on Boeing go back fifty-one years. If you had owned Boeing on December 31, 1961 until the end of 2012 your total annual return would be about 15.8%. If you had owned this stock the past fourteen years you would have beaten the major market averages. Boeing has always paid a dividend during this time frame and the current dividend rate going forward is in the 2.5% range. This would have been a bumpy ride, but the return would be better than the market average. I have never owned Boeing but if I were to buy it I would wait for an approximately 30% to 40% drop from the recent high before buying it. Take a good look at Spreadsheet 9.3. If you had bought Boeing after one or two bad years in a row you would have done very well in the following periods.

Picking a Market Bottom

Pro Shares Ultra S&P 500 (SSO)

This is an ETF that is set up to replicate the S&P 500 performance at twice the rate of return of the index. This means if the S&P 500 Index goes up 1% on a given day the fund should go up 2%. It's the same on a down day. If the index goes down 1% the fund should go down by 2%. This ETF even pays a small dividend. This fund is managed using futures and the futures are settled at the end of each day. In 2010 the fund (SSO) had a total return of 26.63% when the S&P 500 fund (SPY) had a total return of 14.84%. This is about 1.8 times the total return of the S&P 500 but its still way better than the S&P 500 Index.

In 2011 the results were a little different. The S&P 500 index ETF (SPY) was basically flat, down 0.04 for the calendar year. However, it did pay dividends and the total return in the SPY index fund was 1.85%. The total return of the fund (SSO) was a negative 3.18%. That's underperforming the market by a total of over 5%. In 2012 the fund (SSO) had a total return of 31.01% to the SPY total return of 15.95%. .

Pro Shares Ultra S&P 600 (SAA)

This fund works exactly the same as the above ETF. This is an ETF that is set up to replicate the S&P 600 Small Cap Index performance at twice the rate of return of the index. This means if the S&P 600 Index goes up 1% on a given day the fund should go up 2%. If the index goes down 1%

the fund should go down by 2%. This ETF has even paid a microscopic dividend. This fund is managed using futures and the futures are settled at the end of each day. In 2010 the fund (SAA) had a total return of 49.95% when the S&P 600 fund (IJR) had a total return of 26.47%. This is about 1.89 times the total return of the S&P 600 ETF fund.

In 2011 the results were much different. The S&P 600 index ETF (IJR) was up less that 1% (0.77%) total return for the calendar year. The total return of the fund (SAA) was a negative 9.35%. That's underperforming the market by a total of over 10% in a flat market. In 2012 the fund (SAA) has a total return of 30.10% compared to the IJR total return of 16.24%

Both of these ETFs (SSO, SAA) can be good tools to use as long as their prospective indexes are headed steadily upward. It's not good to be in either of these issues in a sideways or down market. Excessive volatility during the time period you own these ETFs could also eat into your returns. Take a look at Spreadsheets 9.4 and 9.5 very closely and compare the correlation between each market ETF and the above mentioned Ultra ETF that is supposed to double the performance of the respective market. As you can see from these comparisons, the stated goal of doubling of the market performance does not usually come true.

Spreadsheet 9.1		Ford Motor			Speculative Stocks			Yearly		
Year Ending 31-Dec	Sym	XLY Begin Price	S&P Consumer Div	Discretionary ETF Div Pct	End Price	Gain Loss	Value	Ave Tot Ret	Year End EPS	P/E
1998	F				58.69		1,000	-2.72% 1,000		
1999	F	58.69	1.88	3.20%	53.31	-5.96%	940	973		
2000	F	26.66	3.54	13.29%	23.44	1.23%	952	946	3.62	7.36
2001	F	23.44	1.05	4.48%	15.72	-28.46%	681	921	(2.95)	
2002	F	15.72	0.40	2.54%	9.30	-38.30%	420	896	0.19	82.74
2003	F	9.30	0.40	4.30%	16.00	76.34%	741	871	0.35	26.57
2004	F	16.00	0.40	2.50%	14.64	-6.00%	697	848	1.59	10.06
2005	F	14.64	0.40	2.73%	7.72	-44.54%	386	824	0.86	17.02
2006	F	7.72	0.25	3.24%	7.51	0.52%	388	802	(6.72)	
2007	F	7.51	0.00	0.00%	6.73	-10.39%	348	780	(1.40)	
2008	F	6.73	0.00	0.00%	2.29	-65.97%	118	759	(6.46)	
2009	F	2.29	0.00	0.00%	10.00	336.68%	517	738	0.86	2.66
2010	F	10.00	0.00	0.00%	16.79	67.90%	868	718	1.66	6.02
2011	F	16.79	0.00	0.00%	11.00	-34.48%	569	699	4.94	3.40
2012	F	11.00	0.20	1.82%	12.95	19.55%	680	680		
				DIA	SPY	XLY	2012	Cumul	Fiscal yr end	
			Cumulative	10.68%	8.69%	56.89%	95.39%	5 yr	31-Dec	
			Cumulative	94.13%	95.71%	131.69%	61.82%	10 yr		
			Cumulative	90.91%	46.69%	110.98%	-32.00%	14 yr		

Spreadsheet 9.2 Goodyear Tire — Speculative Stocks

Year Ending 31-Dec	Sym	XLY Begin Price	Div	Div Pct	End Price	Gain Loss	Value	Yearly Ave Tot Ret -7.51%	Year End EPS	P/E
1998	GT				50.44		1,000	1,000		
1999	GT	50.44	1.20	2.38%	28.06	-41.99%	580	925	1.53	32.97
2000	GT	28.06	1.20	4.28%	22.99	-13.79%	500	855	0.25	112.24
2001	GT	22.99	1.02	4.44%	23.81	8.00%	540	791	(1.59)	
2002	GT	23.81	0.48	2.02%	6.81	-69.38%	165	732	(7.47)	
2003	GT	6.81	0.00	0.00%	7.86	15.42%	191	677	(4.60)	
2004	GT	7.86	0.00	0.00%	14.66	86.51%	356	626	0.63	12.48
2005	GT	14.66	0.00	0.00%	17.38	18.55%	422	579	0.66	22.21
2006	GT	17.38	0.00	0.00%	20.99	20.77%	510	535	(2.10)	
2007	GT	20.99	0.00	0.00%	28.22	34.44%	685	495	0.59	35.58
2008	GT	28.22	0.00	0.00%	5.97	-78.84%	145	458	(0.32)	(88.19)
2009	GT	5.97	0.00	0.00%	14.10	136.18%	342	424	(1.55)	
2010	GT	14.10	0.00	0.00%	11.83	-16.10%	287	392	(0.89)	
2011	GT	11.83	0.00	0.00%	14.17	19.78%	344	362	1.18	
2012	GT	14.17	0.00	0.00%	13.81	-2.54%	335	335		
				DIA	SPY	XLY	2012	Cumul	Fiscal yr end	
			Cumulative	10.68%	8.69%	56.89%	-51.06%	5 yr	31-Dec	
			Cumulative	94.13%	95.71%	131.69%	102.79%	10 yr		
			Cumulative	90.91%	46.69%	110.98%	-66.46%	14 yr		

Spreadsheet 9.3 The Boeing Company — Speculative Stocks

Year Ending 31-Dec	Sym	XLI Begin Price	Div	Div Pct	End Price	Gain Loss	Value	Yearly Ave Tot Ret 8.25%	Year End EPS	P/E
1998	BA				32.63		1,000	1,000		
1999	BA	32.63	0.56	1.72%	41.44	28.72%	1,287	1,082	2.49	13.10
2000	BA	41.44	0.56	1.35%	66.00	60.62%	2,067	1,172	2.44	16.98
2001	BA	66.00	0.68	1.03%	38.78	-40.21%	1,236	1,268	3.41	19.35
2002	BA	38.78	0.68	1.75%	32.99	-13.18%	1,073	1,373	2.84	13.65
2003	BA	32.99	0.68	2.06%	42.14	29.80%	1,393	1,486	0.85	38.81
2004	BA	42.14	0.77	1.83%	51.77	24.68%	1,737	1,609	2.24	18.81
2005	BA	51.77	1.00	1.93%	70.24	37.61%	2,390	1,741	3.19	16.23
2006	BA	70.24	1.20	1.71%	88.84	28.19%	3,064	1,885	2.84	24.73
2007	BA	88.84	1.40	1.58%	87.46	0.02%	3,064	2,041	5.26	16.89
2008	BA	87.46	1.60	1.83%	42.67	-49.38%	1,551	2,209	3.65	23.96
2009	BA	42.67	1.68	3.94%	54.13	30.79%	2,029	2,391	1.87	22.82
2010	BA	54.13	1.68	3.10%	65.26	23.67%	2,509	2,588	4.45	12.16
2011	BA	65.26	1.68	2.57%	73.35	14.97%	2,884	2,802	5.33	12.24
2012	BA	73.35	1.76	2.40%	75.36	5.14%	3,033	3,033		
				DIA	SPY	XLI	2012	Cumul	Fiscal yr end	
			Cumulative	10.68%	8.69%	8.61%	-1.03%	5 yr	31-Dec	
			Cumulative	94.13%	95.71%	122.15%	182.58%	10 yr		
			Cumulative	90.91%	46.69%	98.08%	203.26%	14 yr		

Spreadsheet 9.4   Speculative ETFs

Year Ending 31-Dec	Sym	Begin Price	Div	Div Pct	End Price	SSO Gain Loss	SSO Value 1,000	SPY Gain Loss	SPY Value 1,000	Percent Difference
		ProShares Ultra S&P 500								
2006							1,000		1,000	
2007	SSO	86.30	1.134	1.31%	82.80	-2.74%	973	5.15%	1,052	7.89%
2008	SSO	82.80	0.561	0.68%	26.27	-67.60%	315	-36.42%	669	31.18%
2009	SSO	26.27	0.293	1.11%	38.24	46.68%	462	26.05%	843	-20.63%
2010	SSO	38.24	0.374	0.98%	48.05	26.63%	585	14.84%	968	-11.79%
2011	SSO	48.05	0.259	0.54%	46.39	-2.92%	568	1.85%	986	4.77%
2012	SSO	46.39	0.425	0.92%	60.35	31.01%	745	15.95%	1,143	-15.06%
					From	To	SSO	Total Re	SPY	
			Cumulative		1-Jan-12	31-Dec-12	31.01%	1 yr	15.95%	
			Cumulative		1-Jan-11	31-Dec-12	27.19%	2 yr	18.10%	
			Cumulative		1-Jan-10	31-Dec-12	61.06%	3 yr	35.62%	
			Cumulative		1-Jan-09	31-Dec-12	136.24%	4 yr	70.95%	
			Cumulative		1-Jan-08	31-Dec-12	-23.45%	5 yr	8.69%	
			Cumulative		1-Jan-07	31-Dec-12	-25.55%	6 yr	14.29%	

Spreadsheet 9.5   Speculative ETFs

Year Ending 31-Dec	Sym	Begin Price	Div	Div Pct	End Price	SSA Gain Loss	SSA Value 1,000	IJR Gain Loss	IJR Value 1,000	Percent Difference
		ProShares Ultra S&P SmallCap 600								
2007							1,000		1,000	
2008	SAA	60.08	0.224	0.37%	22.60	-62.01%	380	-31.36%	686	30.65%
2009	SAA	22.60	0.048	0.21%	30.93	37.07%	521	25.67%	863	-11.40%
2010	SAA	30.93	0.010	0.03%	46.37	49.95%	781	26.47%	1,091	-23.48%
2011	SAA	46.37	0.043	0.09%	41.99	-9.35%	708	0.77%	1,099	10.12%
2012	SAA	41.99	0.027	0.07%	54.60	30.10%	921	16.24%	1,278	-13.86%
					From	To	SSA	Total Re	IJR	
			Cumulative		1-Jan-12	31-Dec-12	30.10%	1 yr	16.24%	
			Cumulative		1-Jan-11	31-Dec-12	17.93%	2 yr	17.14%	
			Cumulative		1-Jan-10	31-Dec-12	76.84%	3 yr	48.14%	
			Cumulative		1-Jan-09	31-Dec-12	142.39%	4 yr	86.17%	
			Cumulative		1-Jan-08	31-Dec-12	-7.92%	5 yr	27.79%	

CHAPTER TEN
ALTERNATIVE INVESTMENTS

Day Trading
Yes, we can understand why some otherwise very intelligent and very talented person could be tempted by all the slick advertizing to get into day trading. Especially, if you were recently downsized out of your career and have had a tough time finding a job that matches your talents. My advice is don't ***do it***, because in all probability you will only make things worse. With all the computerized trading going on in the markets today, the individual investor sitting at home with his own computer doesn't have much of a chance against the much more sophisticated computer systems at the major brokerages that are also day trading.

If you are tempted to day trade, please go back to Chapter 5, paragraph 2 and read it again and again and again until the temptation goes away.

Hedge Funds
One way to get close to day trading without actually doing it is to invest in a hedge fund. A typical hedge fund will charge that typical 1% of assets under their management. In addition, the managers also want 20% of the profits from your account. Hedge funds are volatile and very high risk. According to a recent 'Fund of Information' article in Barron's: Through the first ten months of 2012 the S&P 500 Index was up about 12% whereas the average hedge fund's return was just 4.8% before their much higher than normal fees. Going forward, a hedge fund would have to outperform by a huge amount just to get you back to even with the S&P 500. That will not happen without a lot more risk of even more losses.

Pension Buyout Offer

If you are like me, an older person who worked enough years with one company to be getting a traditional (defined benefit annuity) pension, you could get *an offer to* buy you out of your pension. By now you know your author can be very skeptical and this situation would be no exception. Just recently in my industry (Automotive Manufacturing), this situation has made the news at least twice. Both Ford and General Motors have made pension buyout offers to some of their salaried retirees. According to a recent article in the New York Times, General Motors has also said it might discuss pension buyouts for its 400,000 hourly retirees and surviving spouses with their union, the United Automobile Workers (UAW).

Regardless of what industries you might work (or have worked) in, keep in mind that, if you are vested in a pension, you will very likely be hearing more and more about similar offers in the next few years. First, you should consider how well you will be able to manage your affairs when you are much older. If you become incapacitated, do you have a *trusted family member or friend* who would be **willing and able** to step in and manage that portfolio for you? That pension buyout money could become a burden because, if you take the pension buyout, it would be up to you to manage all of your financial assets. Without the buyout you always have the pension to fall back on if the market doesn't go your way. No one should tell you not to take such an offer if received. If you do decide to take such an offer you should have a well thought out plan in place to cover any contingency.

Immediate Annuities

It's almost certain that with the pension buyout offers we are going to see in the near future, one option you will hear about from insurance companies is an offer of an immediate annuity. This is basically a pension that you can buy yourself with a lump sum of money. This is one way for you to easily compare a pension buyout offer. Currently, a typical offer for a 65 year old male, with no heirs, is about $548 per month for a $100,000 lump sum non refundable deposit. Even though we are living longer than in the past, interest rates are at record lows and this will keep offers low until interest rates rise. You can check for the latest offers based on you and your spouse's age at www.immediateannuities.com.

AFTERWORD

I want to dedicate this book to all the working people in America who are now responsible for managing their own retirement accounts. In the last thirty years working people have been squeezed from all sides. Defined benefit pension plans have been mismanaged and underfunded in many cases just to pay upper management huge bonuses. Many of the powers that be now want to blame the victims and offer only a meager 401k plan in their place.

Even though we have paid into Social Security and Medicare our whole working lives the benefits we were promised are coming under attack. More and more responsibility for our future has been thrust upon us whether we like it or not. If you do not take personal control of your assets by the time you get to retirement you could easily have given away unnecessarily 10% or more of your net worth to financial planners and investment advisors.

In conclusion, in writing my first book but maybe not my last, if just one person is kept from making a catastrophic financial mistake it will be well worth all the time and effort put forth in writing this book. You are welcome to contact me by email at cwemery@yahoo.com with your questions or comments.

I accepted Jesus Christ as my Lord and Savior on April 4, 2010.

INDEX

Page references with italicized "*n*" refer to footnote references.
Page references with italicized "*ill*" or "*ills*" refer to spreadsheets.

Numbers
401k/403b (defined contribution plans)
　decisions in, 1
　vs. discount brokerage account, 3
　investing in employer sponsored, 11–14
　rolling over money from, 12

A
Abbott Labs (ABT), 64, 77*ill*
Air Products and Chemicals (APD), 62, 74*ill*
Alerian MLP Exchange Traded Fund (ETF) (AMLP), 82
Alerian MLP Index, 85
All-or-None Order, 51
alternative investments, 107–8
Altria (Philip Morris) (MO), 59, 67*ill*
American Depositary Receipts (ADRs), 50
American Electric Power (AEP), 64, 79*ill*
American Greed (CNBC), 4
AmeriGas Partners (APU), 88*ill*
annuities, immediate, 108
Apple (AAPL), 38
AT&T (T), 63, 76*ill*
auto industry, 97–100
averaging down, 54–55

B
banks, charging custody fees, 50
Barron's (newspaper), 6, 50
Barron's—Zack's ranking of brokers' stock pick lists, 6
BB&T Bank (BBT), 61, 71*ill*, 95
Bid/Asked spread, 50-51
Big Three Automakers, 2008 meltdown, 97–100
Boards of Directors, of mutual funds, 23
The Boeing Company (BA), 101, 103*ill*
bond issues not rated, 91
bonds
　laddering, 92
　vs. preferred stocks, 93
Bonds Screener, on Yahoo finance, 2
Boston Market, 52
Britain, taxing dividends, 50
brokerage firms
　accounts, 2
　commissions, 3, 5
brokerage industry, regulation of, 5–6
brokers, discount, 2, 3

Buckeye Partners (BPL), 87*ill*
Buffett, Warren, 52
business cycle
  about, 25
  defensive, 27
  final, 27–28
  recovery, 27
  sectors of S&P 500, 25, 29*ill*
  spreadsheets for performance of business sectors, 30–35*ills*

C

capitalization weighted indexes., 39
Center for Responsive Politics, 3
Cerberus, 99
Chevron (CVX), 59–60, 68*ill*
China, investing in, 41
Chrysler, 97–99
Citigroup (C), 61, 72*ill*
CNBC
  American Greed, 4
  "Mad Money," 49
college tuition costs, paying, 2
commissions and fees
  401k/403b, 11
  broker, 3
  financial advisors, 4–5
  mutual funds, 11, 19–20
common stocks
  All-or-None Order, 51
  averaging down, 54–55
  building portfolio of, 49
  derived from SPDR Nine ETFs, 55–58. *see also individual stocks*
  Dividend Reinvestment Plans, 54
  Fill-or-Kill-Order, 51
  General Electric, 54–55
  growth stocks vs. dividend paying stocks, 53
  Initial Public Offerings, 52
  limit vs. market orders, 51
  purchasing employer, 12–13
  system of, 50–51
  value investing, 51–52
Congress, lobbyists in, 3
ConocoPhillips (COP), 60, 69*ill*
corporate bonds, 91
Cramer, Jim, 49, 99
cumulative preferred stock, 94
custody fees, transfer agents and banks charging, 50

D

day trading, 3–4, 107
defensive business cycle, 27
defined benefit pensions, 1
defined contribution plans (401k/403b)
  vs. 401k/403b, 3
  decisions in, 1
  investing in employer sponsored, 11–14
  rolling over money from, 12
  spreadsheets for estimating contributions, 15–16*ills*
DIA, Dow Industrials S&P 500 ETF, 25, 29*ill*, 40
discount broker, commissions, 5
discount brokers, accounts, 2
dividend paying stocks vs. growth stocks, 53
Dividend Reinvestment Plans (DRIPS), 54
dividends
  preferred stocks and, 94, 95
  taxes and fees connected to common stock, 50
DJIA (Dow Jones Industrial Average)
  number of times changed, 40
  vs. S&P 500 Index, 38, 40–41

spreadsheet for performance of, 45*ill*
"don't invest in something you don't understand," cliché, 37
Dow Industrials S&P 500 ETF (DIA), 25, 29*ill*, 40
Dow Jones Industrial Average (DJIA)
   number of times changed, 40
   vs. S&P 500 Index, 38, 40–41
   spreadsheet for performance of, 45*ill*
DRIPS (Dividend Reinvestment Plans), 54
DuPont (DD), 63, 75*ill*

E

Edwards, John, 5
Emerson Electric (EMR), 62, 73*ill*
employer sponsored 401k/403b, 11–17
Energy Transfer Partners (ETP), 86*ill*
ETNs (Exchange Traded Notes)
   companies to invest in to avoid K-1s, 82
   vs. ETFs, 82–83
Exchange Traded Funds (ETFs). *see also* S&P 500 Index ETFs
   about, 37
   beating the indexes, 42–43
   in defensive business cycle, 27
   vs. ETNs, 82–83
   in final business cycle, 27–28
   to follow, 39–40
   gold, 43-44
   investing in Master Limited Partnerships, 82
   leading stocks derived from SPDR Nine, 55–58. *see also individual stocks*
   vs. mutual funds, 2, 20–23
   performance calculations, 41–42
   in recovery business cycle, 27
   speculation, 97
   speculative, 104*ill*
   style investing, 44
   system of buying and selling, 50–51
   using total return of, 14
Exchange Traded Notes (ETNs), 82-83

F

Facebook (FB), 52
fall of 2008, 91, 97–100
Federal Reserve Board, and short term interest rates, 93
fee only financial planners, xi
fees and commissions
   401k/403b, 11–13
   broker, 3
   financial advisors, 4–5
   mutual funds, 11, 19–23
Fill-or-Kill-Order, 51
final business cycle, 27–28
financial advisors
   fees charged by, 4–5
   obligation of, xi
FINRA (Financial Industry Regulatory Authority), 5–6
first home, purchasing, 2
fixed income, 91–95
Ford, William Clay, Jr., 98
Ford Motor (F), 97–100, 102*ill*, 108
foreign markets, investing in, 41
Fox News, political commentary of, 49
France, taxing dividends, 50

G

General Electric (GE), 54, 62, 72*ill*
General Mills (GIS), 59, 68*ill*
General Motors, 98–99, 108

gold ETFs, 43-44
Goodyear Tire (GT), 100, 103*ill*
Government Treasuries U.S., 91
Groupon Inc. (GRPN), 52
growth stocks vs. dividend paying stocks, 53

H
Health Care REIT (HCN), 61, 70*ill*
hedge funds, 107
Hulbert's Financial Digest (newsletter), 6
hybrid stocks, 92

I
Iacocca, Lee, 99
IJR, S&P 600 Small Cap ETFs, 21, 27
immediate annuities, 108
"In Service Withdrawal," 13
"In the long term it all reverts to the mean," cliché, 26
index funds vs. professionally managed funds, 14
Initial Public Offerings (IPOs), 52
Intel (INTC), 63, 75*ill*
intra-day trading, 22
investment portfolio, spreadsheets, 7–8*ills*
Investment Trusts, 19. *see also* mutual funds
investments
    alternative, 107–8
    reasons for managing own, 1
    tracking on Yahoo Finance, 2
IRAs, Regular, rolling over money into, 12–13
IRS form K-1, 82, 84
IRS website, Publication 590 for contributing to Roth IRAs, 3
I-Shares S&P 500 Index (IVV), 21, 23
IVE (S&P Value ETF), 53

IVW (S&P Growth ETF), 53
IWM, Russell 2000 Small Cap ETFs, 27, 39

J
Japan, taxing dividends, 50
Johnson & Johnson (JNJ), 63, 77*ill*
J.P. Morgan-Alerian MLP Index Exchange Traded Note (AMJ), 82

K
K-1s, 82-84
Kinder Morgan Energy Partners (KMP), 87*ill*

L
laddering bonds, 92
large cap blend funds, 21
limit orders vs. market orders, 51
Lipper Mutual Fund averages, 21
lobbyists, in Congress, 3

M
"Mad Money" (CNBC), 49, 99
Magellan Midstream Partners (MMP), 86*ill*
market
    picking bottom of, 101–2
    speculation in, 102–4*ills*
market orders vs. limit orders, 51
Master Limited Partnerships (MLPs), 49, 81–88
McDonald's (MCD), 56–58, 66*ill*
Medicare, 111
meltdown of 2008, 91, 97–100
mid cap index funds, 13–14
Money, MSN, 2
money managers, ranking of, 6
Moody's, Standard & Poor, and Fitch, 91

Morningstar (website), 95
MSN Money, 2
Mulally, Alan, 98, 99
mutual funds
   about, 19
   Boards of Directors of, 23
   choosing, 13–14
   disclosure requirements of, 22
   vs. ETFs, 2, 20–23
   fees charged by, 11, 19–20
   liability of advisors for false statements on, 4
   Lipper Mutual Fund averages, 21
   management of, 20
   names of, 21–22
   taxes paid by, 20–21
   turnover rates of, 20

N
Nardelli, Bob, 99
NASDAQ Composite Index, 26
Ned Davis Research, dividend paying vs. growth stocks, 53
Net Asset Value (NAV), 22
New York Stock Exchange (NYSE), shares of stock changing hands on, 3
New Zealand, taxing dividends, 50
1986 Tax Reform Act, Master Limited Partnerships in, 81
non-cumulative preferred stock, 94
NuStar Energy LP (NS), 88*ill*
NYSE (New York Stock Exchange), shares of stock changing hands on, 3

O
Obama, Barack, 98
on line stock trading, 2
ONEOK, 64

P
pension buyout offers, 108
pensions, defined benefit, 1
performance, reverting to mean, 26
Philip Morris (Altria) (MO), 59, 67*ill*
Pitney Bowes (PB), 49–50
portfolios, tracking, 2
preferred stocks, 49, 92–95
Pro Shares Ultra S&P 500 (SSO), 101–2, 104*ill*
Pro Shares Ultra S&P 600 (SAA), 101–2, 104*ill*
Proctor & Gamble (PG), 38, 59, 67*ill*
professionally managed funds vs. index funds, 14
purchasing first home, 2

R
rating of corporate bonds, 91–92
Realty Income (O), 60, 70*ill*
recovery business cycle, 27
Regular IRAs, rolling over money into, 12–13
return of capital, and taxes, 82
rolling over money
   from 401k/403b plan, 12
   into Regular IRAs, 12–13
Roth IRAs
   eligibility for contributing to, 2–3
   Master Limited Partnerships and, 84
   taxing, 12
   withdrawing funds from, 2
Royal Dutch Shell (RDS-B), 55, 55*n*, 60, 69*ill*
RPM International, 74*ill*
RPM International (RPM), 62, 74*ill*
Russell 2000 Small Cap ETFs, IWM, 27, 39

Russell 2000 Small Cap Index, performance of, 14, 17*ill*
Rydex Equal Weight S&P 500 ETF (RSP), 26, 29*ill*, 38, 46*ill*

S

S&P 1500 Dividend Aristocrats (SDY), 53
S&P 400 Mid Cap ETFs, IJH, 21
S&P 500 Index. *see also* Exchange Traded Funds (ETFs)
   about, 38
   on companies paying dividends in, 50
   vs. Dow Jones Industrial Average, 38, 40–41
   sectors of, 25, 29*ill*
   vs. The SPDR Nine performance, 26
S&P 500 Index ETFs
   Dow Industrials (DIA), 25, 29*ill*, 40-41
   I-Shares (IVV), 21, 23
   Rydex Equal Weight (RSP), 26, 29*ill*, 38, 46*ill*
   SPDR (SPY). *see* SPY, SPDR S&P 500 ETF
S&P 600 Small Cap ETFs, IJR, 21, 27
S&P 600 Small Cap Index, performance of, 14, 17*ill*
S&P Growth ETF (IVW), 53
S&P Value ETF (IVE), 53
Scottrade, 37
Securities and Exchange Commission (SEC)
   on mutual fund fees, 19
   protection of investors by, 4, 6
shares of stock
   changing hands on NYSE, 3
   day trading, 3–4
Shell Oil (Royal Dutch Shell), 55, 55*n*, 60, 69*ill*
short term interest rates, 93
small cap index funds, 14
Smart Money (magazine), on rolling over money into Regular IRAs, 13
Social Security, 111
Southern Company (SO), 64, 78*ill*
The SPDR Nine
   in defensive business cycle, 27
   leading stocks derived from, 55–58. *see also individual stocks*
   performance of, 25–28, 42–43
   in recovery business cycle, 27
   spreadsheets for performance of, 29–35*ills*
speculation, 97, 97–102, 102–4*ills*
Spread, 50--51
spreadsheets
   for estimating contribution amounts on 401k/403b, 15–16*ills*
   investment portfolio, 4–5, 7–8*ills*
SPY, SPDR S&P 500 ETF
   vs. large cap blend funds, 21
   leading stocks derived from, 55–58. *see also individual stocks*
   vs. performance of mutual funds, 23
   vs. The SPDR Nine performance, 25–26, 29*ill*, 42–43
Standard and Poor. *see also* S&P 500 Index, as rating agency, 91
state income taxes, 84
stock broker, obligation of, xi
stock trading
   All-or-None Order, 51
   averaging down, 54–55

Dividend Reinvestment Plans, 54
Fill-or-Kill-Order, 51
growth stocks vs. dividend paying stocks, 53
Initial Public Offerings, 52
leading stocks derived from SPDR Nine ETFs, 55–58. *see also individual stocks*
limit vs. market orders, 51
on line, 2
on NYSE, 3
S&P 1500 Dividend Aristocrats, 53
speculation, 97–104
system of, 50–51
value investing, 51–52
stocks
   day trading, 107
   growth stocks vs. dividend paying stocks, 53
   hybrid, 92
   leading stocks derived from SPDR Nine ETFs, 55–58. *see also individual stocks*
   pick lists of brokers, 6
   preferred, 49, 92–95
   speculation in, 97–104
   using total return of, 14
style investing, 44
suitable investments, xi

T
tax deferred accounts, Master Limited Partnerships and, 84
taxes
   paid by mutual funds, 20–21
   return of capital and, 82
   Roth IRA account and, 12
   on stock dividends, 50
TD Ameritrade, 51

"The best time to buy is when there's blood in the streets," cliché, 43, 97
total returns chart, 56
trading symbols, of preferred stock, 95
transfer agents, charging custody fees, 50
2008 meltdown, 91, 97–98

U
UBS E-TRACS Alerian MLP Infrastructure ETN (MLPI), 84
UBS E-TRACS Alerian Natural Gas MLP Index ETN (MLPG), 84
United Automobile Workers (UAW), 98, 108
United Parcel Service (UPS), 62, 73*ill*
Unrelated Business Taxable Income (UBTI), 84
U.S. Government Treasuries, 91

V
value investing, 51–52
Vanguard S&P 500 Index Fund (VFINX), 13
Verizon (VZ), 63, 76*ill*
VF Corporation (VFC), 58, 66*ill*

W
Wagoner, Rick, 98
Wall Street brokerages, broker commissions, 3
Washington DC, lobbyists in, 3
Wells Fargo (WFC), 61, 71*ill*
Westar Energy (WR), 65, 79*ill*

Y
Yahoo Finance
   Bonds Screener on, 2
   tracking investments on, 2

Yield to Worst (YTW), 93

Z
Zack's, Barron's—, ranking of brokers' stock pick lists, 6

www.ingramcontent.com/pod-product-compliance
Lightning Source LLC
Chambersburg PA
CBHW030810180526
45163CB00003B/1225